CURRIER'S QUICK A

WARMWATER [...]NG

BY JEFF CURRIER

To Steve,

It's always great to meet folks
that like to fly fish for <u>All</u> species.
I look forward to trying your flies!

Jeff Currier

San Mateo
"2006"

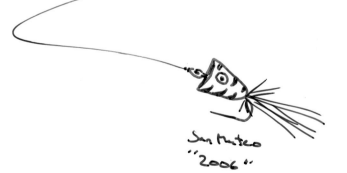

ILLUSTRATIONS & PHOTOGRAPHS BY JEFF CURRIER

FLY IMAGES BY DAVID J. SWIFT

FOREWORD BY SCOTT SANCHEZ

Jeff Currier
P.O. Box 3548
Jackson, WY 83001
(307) 733-3270

Editor: Bud Bynack
Design & Layout: 5640 Design, Alpine, WY
Printer: Ink On Paper - www.ink-on-paper.com

Printed in the United States of America

ISBN# 0-9721258-0-9

Print number 10 9 8 7 6 5 4 3 2 1

LIBRARY OF CONGRESS CONTROL NUMBER : 2002093649

Dedicated to my wife Yvonne – she lets me fish all the time. I better not push it or she might hit me with a wet carp . . . and this burly mirror carp would really hurt!

CONTENTS

ILLUSTRATIONS & PHOTOGRAPHS

ACKNOWLEDGEMENTS

This book is dedicated to my wife Yvonne who unlike most wives never disrupts my extreme fishing habits. Not only am I free to fish on every non working day of my life, but she gives me two entire rooms in our house, one for storing and organizing freshwater tackle, and one for storing and organizing saltwater tackle. That's not to mention the muddy waders lumped in the corner of the entry way, the permanently set up fly tying vise in the living room, the fly boxes on the kitchen table, or the car in the driveway because the boat is in the garage. She is my closest friend and best fishing companion.

I must thank my family. My father Charles took me fishing at a very early age. My mother Sue, brother Greg and his wife Kerry, and sister Becky and her husband Don Rose are not only fishing companions, but are amazing supporters of my fishing career. Then there is my late grandfather Wesley Currier whom owned our family cottage on Lake Winnipesaukee in New Hampshire. When I was a kid he never once ignored my requests of, "Grampy, let's go fishing", which were not a few occasional times, but rather more than half of every childhood summer to chase smallmouth by day and bullhead by night. I spent nearly the same amount of time fishing out of the cottage with my cousins Jon, Rob, and Jay Blake, and Mark Pierce as well as my boyhood best friend, Joe Jones. Between the six of us we tormented more chain pickerel of Back Bay than any group of anglers could catch in a lifetime!

I am honored to have the Foreword of this book written by Scott Sanchez. Scott is the wholesale manager of Dan Bailey's in Livingston, Montana and a freelance writer for many publications worldwide. He is undoubtedly the finest and most creative fly tier whom I have ever met, and his help with Appendix B contributing many of the flies and their recipes was an asset. Scott's knowledge of tackle, trout, warmwater fish species, and saltwater fish species, surpasses that of most other experts in the field. Scott is a long time friend and usually the first person I call for advice, input, or simply expertise on any fishing subject.

I would like to thank my employer, Jack Dennis, author of three very popular fly tying manuals, producer of many fine instructional fly tying and fishing videos, and owner of the Jack Dennis Outdoor Shop. It was his example that sparked my initiative to write books in the first place. My immediate boss, Larry Bashford, the general manager of the Jack Dennis Outdoor Shop also needs to be credited for allowing me time to travel and fish. Few bosses would let any employee take off as much time as I have over the years. Then there are my present and past work companions. Chris Jay, Bruce James, Mike Patron, Mike Spessard, Greg Allen, Clif

Williams, Jennifer Kocher, Scott Smith, David Block, Mike Jansen, Rob Merrill, Brandon Powers, and Jim Reetz not only tested my knot tying instructions, but kept up the quality control on all my art work and photographs used throughout this book. Like family, they have been tremendous supporters of my work.

Special thanks are required to those who hosted me on excursions for research and assisted with photographs for this book. Close friend Kevin Hunter of Fairhope, Alabama generously donated not only couch space, but also his time. Kevin fished, held fish, and modeled for me from dawn to dusk for five straight days and introduced me to Manley Cummins, owner of an incredible private lake, and his friend Kit Smith. Manley and Kit are two of the finest largemouth bass anglers I've ever met.

Jack and Marsha Modesett deserve equal recognition for bringing my wife and me to Texas to fish their own private water. I have never seen poppers bring out burley largemouth bass with such regularity!

Friend John Jazwa turned me on to some incredible striped bass fishing on Elephant Butte Reservoir in New Mexico with guide Bobby Brewster. Long time fishing partner John Keener showed me a bit of everything from freshwater drum to yellow bass throughout Illinois, and Don Ambrose, a native of Wisconsin, treated me many times to some of the finest muskellunge fishing left on the world! In fact, all my Northland College colleagues, Paul Beriger, Mark Rieser, Dave Kittaka, Tim Santel, Andy Thompson, Mike Newman, and Matt Norton, compile an enormous amount of knowledge about catching the many warmwater species of the Midwest. They have always been eager to share this knowledge and are thus great fishing buddies.

A special thanks goes to Ben Smith and Trey Scharp who traveled over 15 hours with me for a mere two day trip to fly fish for and photograph northern pike of Colorado's Yampa River. Close friend Adam Cohen, who has since tragically lost his life to cancer, joined me in one of the most adventurous months of my life throughout El Salvador, Honduras, and Nicaragua in which we fly fished and photographed guapote, mojarra, and machaca. Derek Mitchell accompanied me to Lake Arenal in Costa Rica where Jimmy Nix and Peter Gorinsky exploited us to monster guapote, and thanks goes to Paul Melchior who got me in touch with Chuck Abernathy of Panama who guided me to my first tight line with a peacock bass. Mike Fitzgerald Jr., Bill Goehring, and Joe Cod of Frontiers International have been an asset to all my exotic travels in search of optimum fishing opportunities.

Brian Horn, one of the finest anglers I know, (he fishes 360 days a year) deserves special thanks for accompanying me and helping me photograph and develop fly fishing techniques for one of South America's toughest gamefish, the payara. His patience through an adventurous excursion throughout Venezuela lead to a successful finish. We not only conquered world record sized payara, but also 10 other exotic freshwater species from pavon to piranha. It must be known that it was not just Brian and I. Glenn Webb, part owner of Laguna Larga fishing camp, got us in touch with Jim Johnston and Linda Sonderman of Alpi Tour in Venezuela. Jim and his Toyota Land Cruiser lead us safely for ten days of fishing through the Llanos of the Orinoco.

Fishing trips alone didn't make this book possible. Quality equipment was essential in catching the many warmwater fish species. Mike Atwell, Skip Gibson, Bob Swan, Brooks Montgomery, Chris Hart, and Dave Rice, who, between them represent some of the finest fly fishing tackle in the industry, have always helped to outfit me with rods, reels, tippets and flies. Lon Deckard, owner of Thomas & Thomas Fly Rod Company sponsored much of my research by making certain I had the necessary rods for every excursion, and Kevin Thompson, of the Sage Rod Company, as well as Jim Bartschi of the Scott Rod Company, are always eager to let me test a new rod on an exotic fish. K. C. Walsh, owner of Simms always helps dress me for cold weather fishing while Bill Wotkyns, owner of Tarponwear keeps me dressed cool in the jungle. Tom McCullough and Marty Downy of the Cortland Line Company have always made sure my reels were full with the latest and greatest of fly lines and backing, and Peter Crow of Action Optic Polarized Sunglasses always makes sure that I see the fish.

Lastly, I thank those who put in many hours of time seeing through the publication of this book. I applaud Bud Bynack, the copyeditor, for diligently reading through my first final draft. His careful attention to every sentence helped create this quality finish. And once again, a standing ovation for Stan and Glenda Bradshaw, for their final edits and for testing the thoroughness of my information. I greatly appreciate their assistance and patience with my second book.

Unfortunately, there is not enough time to chase the warmwater species with everyone. However friends like Paul Bruun, Tom Montgomery, Ed and Pat Opler, Gary Lafontaine, John Bailey, Mike Lawson, Jay Buchner, Joe Burke, Brad Befus, Lee and Boyd Erickson, Rob Waters, and Will Dornan have been a great help over the years with advice and support on a career in fly fishing.

It would be impossible to mention all the people and friends that had at least some influence on this book or my experiences fly fishing for warmwater species. Those of you who are not mentioned know who you are, and I cannot thank you enough.

-JEFF CURRIER, May 2002

FOREWORD

Ever since I've known Jeff, he has been fanatical about fishing, and it shows in his skill and insight. Jeff will fish anywhere for anything. There probably isn't a place or situation when he wouldn't at least investigate a fishing opportunity. He is always looking for new adventures. I worked with Jeff at Jack Dennis Outdoor Shop for a number of years, and we have stayed in close contact.

When we first met fifteen years ago, Jeff had just graduated from Northland College in Wisconsin and spent a summer working in Yellowstone National Park. It didn't take long to figure out he would be an asset to the stores fishing department. Besides his knowledge of Yellowstone waters, he had some great stories of warmwater fishing during college and while growing up in Massachusetts. When I tried to get him to go hunting in the fall, he would decline, because it would cut into his fishing time. Since then, we've fished, taught clinics, made presentations, worked sports shows, and put down a few beers together. We have had some great times chasing local trout, trying to track down bass in Wyoming, and fishing saltwater.

During a couple of years I spent in Texas, I actually had a chance to spend a little more recreational time with him. During the years we worked together, it was difficult to fish together. Being the two top hands at Jack's meant different days off. When I talked to him on the phone from Texas, he would update me on the trout fishing, and I would give him details of my bass, striper, and redfishing. Both of us had some great vicarious fishing. During those winters, I helped Jeff out with a Jack Dennis booth at sports shows. If we had the chance, we'd fish. During a San Mateo, California, show, we fished almost every night. The plan was to have me crank out the flies we needed at the booth, leave the show as soon as possible and blast down to the Berkeley Pier. We got some strange looks throwing shooting heads off the pier, but we had fun, and Jeff managed to catch a baby striper and a small kingfish (croaker).

Jeff looks at the different varieties of fly fishing as just fishing. He is wise enough to realize that although each type of angling has its own elements, there is a great deal of knowledge that can be transferred from one type of fishing to others. He can be happy chasing whatever is available. One of his passions is topwater. Whether he is drifting a small dry on the Henry's Fork, using a diver for pike, teasing piranhas, or throwing poppers at cudas, he loves the thrill of visual takes.

Every time we talk, he is off on a new adventure and it is always enjoyable to hear about his latest trip. Payara and peacocks in Venezuela, roosters in Baja, Rainbow Bass in Nicaragua, machaca in Costa Rica, or carp in Idaho, Jeff and the flies I've given him to try have enough stamps on their passport to make most people envious. Jeff's testing of my flies has led to the evolution of some of them. He once caught a world record channel catfish on my Double Bunny.

Very few people have the skills to write, photograph, and illustrate their own fly fishing book. Jeff does, and in addition, he has a wide range of practical angling skills. He draws from this knowledge to demonstrate logical techniques. I didn't realize he had artistic talents until one day he showed me a painting he was working on. I was impressed. He provided many of the illustrations used in the book *Tying with Jack Dennis and Friends*. His first book *Currier's Quick and Easy Guide to Saltwater Fly Fishing* has helped many anglers prepare for their first saltwater trip. His great photos have graced the pages of national magazines. These abilities give him an edge in conveying his thoughts to the reader. He is passionate about his fishing, but he isn't a snob. He will go out of his way to help a struggling neophyte, and he is an excellent teacher. This warmwater book will introduce anglers to the great sport found in warmwater fly fishing.

-Scott Sanchez
Livingston, Montana
April 2001

No barriers keep Scott Sanchez from chasing the fish.

INTRODUCTION

Few fly fishers take advantage of the fish species that are closest to home. I have worked at the Jack Dennis Fly Shop in Jackson Hole, Wyoming, for over fifteen years and have been fortunate to meet all types of fly-fishing men and women from across the globe. Many are envious of where I make my living, claiming that there is no fly fishing where they come from. For few is this true. Nearly any spot in the world offers at least one species of fish that will readily eat a well-presented fly and prove to be a challenge to land on the appropriate fly rod and line weight.

Take for example the carp, regarded as a "junk fish" by nearly all except an elite group of wise anglers. Yet the carp can make even the most cautious brown trout seem gullible, and once hooked can take normal freshwater equipment to the brink of breaking every time.

The objective of *Currier's Quick and Easy Guide to Warmwater Fly Fishing* is to teach anglers how to appreciate these often ignored fish species and how to pursue them with a fly rod. It is information that I have accumulated after a lifetime of on-the-water experience, learning from my own mistakes and from the experiences of other anglers and guides. I have explained and illustrated the various water types and conditions you are most apt to meet, the equipment, knots, and techniques that you will need to know to get started, as well as the methods for targeting many warmwater species.

As you progress in warmwater fly fishing, you will come to realize that there are many ways to approach the same situation. For example, experienced warmwater fly fishers may disagree about whether top-water flies or subsurface flies are the preferred way to fool weary largemouth bass, or whether to fish wire or heavy monofilament for shock tippets for northern pike, or what fly rod lengths are best for float tubing. In fact, there are many ways to reach the same goal. In order to simplify things for the beginning warmwater fly fisher, however, I have narrowed the scope of options to those that have worked for me. As you get further into the sport, you will likely want to experiment with other techniques and approaches, and you should. That's part of the fun.

The largemouth bass is one of America's favorite gamefish. Why not catch it on a fly?

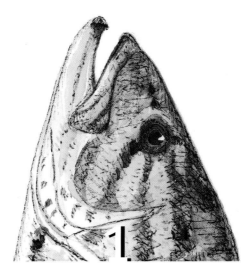

WHY WARMWATER FLY FISHING?

With all the great fly fishing throughout the world for trout and the growing passion of saltwater fly fishing, why would anyone want to land a one-pound bluegill or strip flies down deep for walleyes on a cold, windy lake?

There are a number of good reasons. One is to escape the crowds that are often found at today's finer fly-fishing destinations. Most of the bodies of fresh water contained by six of the earth's seven continents are inhabited by warmwater fish species. Therefore, the opportunities to fish are plentiful. Easy-to-reach locations throughout the world may be only a block away from wherever you are. For instance, carp thrive in city park ponds, and in the United States, these locations often produce bluegills, crappies, bass, and channel catfish, as well.

Warmwater fly fishing also provides a very diverse selection of species from which to choose. North America itself may be the finest location of all. Canada offers fishing of legendary quality for northern pike, walleyes, and smallmouth bass. The United States hosts those same species, plus more than a dozen others, and is home to the celebrated largemouth bass. Central America, a mere sliver of land, is home to many cichlids that will absolutely smash a top-water fly, including the widely distributed guapote, a fish known to Americans as the rainbow bass, and the hard-fighting machaca and mojarra. The Amazon Basin of South America holds the peacock bass, which is constantly growing in popularity among fly fishers, plus the freshwater dorado, piranha, payara, and possibly over one hundred more. Australia has its own family of native warmwater fishes known as cod (much different from saltwater cod), as well as its own type of bass and perch. Remote parts of Africa are home to the tigerfish, one of the toothiest of all fishes, and in the Himalayas of Asia lives the mahseer, a member of the carp family that grows to over one hundred pounds.

As one can imagine, the tremendous varieties of warmwater species worldwide offer many unique challenges. For instance, largemouth bass, one of North America's favorite gamefish, frequently surpass 10 pounds. Trophy fish such as these reside amid structures such as sunken or fallen trees surrounded by lily pads and other vegetation. It's possible for an angler to hook several of these monsters over the course of a lifetime, but pulling one out from such a fortress is nearly impossible. Other species such as the muskellunge not only exceed 50 pounds and lurk in a protected habitat of their own, but also are considered to be among the wiliest fish on earth. Some of northern Wisconsin's oldest and finest bait fishers can count hookups with muskies on one hand.

Although most North American warmwater species are within easy traveling distance, it can take days to reach where monster northern pike lurk in Canada's Northwest Territory. And heading south to the headwaters of the Amazon in Peru entails at least two days of travel. Civil unrest, language barriers, transportation headaches, dysentery, and skimpy information can tack on more time. Once you make it to

Warmwater species thrive in and around most urban regions. Here an angler pursues carp alongside a busy highway.

Warmwater species exist throughout the world. South America's red bellied piranha can provide hours of fun on a 5-weight fly rod, but as you can see, flies don't last very long.

your South American destination, only local guides with a lifetime of experience know the seasonal nuances and fish habits, as well as how to navigate these jungle rivers.

Finally, warmwater fly fishing will challenge your skills. Many situations require casting large, wind-resistant flies with stiff shock tippets. Long and accurate placement of these flies far back under overhanging tree branches or tight against a protruding log can be a must. Ever-present winds contribute to the casting challenge.

Warmwater fly fishing offers something for everyone and fishing opportunities as convenient or as unusual as you could desire, from the bluegill pond in the local park, where anglers can fish after a hard day at work and teach their kids the art, to the exotic species and travel adventures to be found by fishing the Amazon, the world's largest river. Warmwater fly-fishing opportunities are as diverse and intriguing as the world itself.

Popping for largemouth bass on a private lake in Alabama.

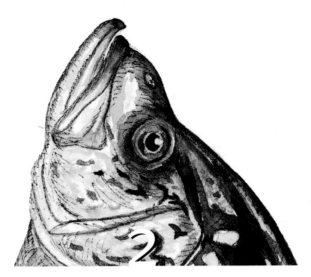

FOUR TYPES OF WATER

An entire book could be written on water types alone if it were really to go into detail and explain differences in places that otherwise might seem similar, such as beaches and sandy points. To keep things simple, however, I will cover the four basic types of water that a newcomer to warmwater fly fishing is likely to encounter. These are ponds, lakes, rivers, and canals. Of course, where and how you fish these waters will vary with a multitude of factors, including the kind of structure that is present, the depth of the water and the depths at which fish hold, currents, if present, and the species of fish you are pursuing. Here, I'll present a quick overview of the tackle and flies appropriate to each kind of water type, topics that I'll go into more detail in later chapters. I'll also sketch some of the safety concerns that each type of water raises. When you're fishing a quiet pond, it's just as important to be safe while having fun as it is when you're taking on the mighty forces of the ocean.

PONDS

Ponds exist in two forms, natural and artificial. Natural ponds are small, shallow bodies of water with aquatic plant life from one shoreline to the other, often bordering or connecting to a marsh or swamp. Lily pads, reeds, cattails, and other emerging vegetation, as well as stumps, trees, beaver dams, and muskrat lodges, often protrude through the surface. Overflowing rivers and heavy rains usually form most natural ponds.

Artificial ponds, often referred to as "tanks" or "pits," are strategically built on farms and ranches for irrigation purposes and to provide drinking water for livestock. They are also commonly constructed for landscaping purposes. Golf courses and housing developments use them worldwide to create a more scenic environment. To enhance the setting, fish are often introduced or arrive naturally through connected rivers and canals. Because many of the warmwater species reside in ponds, I will discuss them first.

Ponds are nearly always rich with life. The shallow water and the scattered debris create hiding places that support populations of many small animals. Insects, snails, freshwater shrimp, leeches, salamanders, frogs, and turtles, to name a few inhabitants, thrive in this environment. These, in turn, attract fish, both big and small. The small fish, mostly minnows and sunfish, dwell in the sunken structure and feed on insects and other tiny animals while hiding from larger fish that come to eat them. That makes ponds great places to pursue warmwater species.

This toad wouldn't stand a chance at swimming across a pond full of largemouth bass and chain pickerel.

Many warmwater species flourish in ponds. Members of the sunfish family, such as largemouth bass, warmouths, bluegills, longear sunfish, and black and white crappies are the best known, but you will also find chain pickerel, northern pike, bowfin, gar, and carp, depending on region and time of year.

The shallow waters of ponds heat up fast in the hot summer sun. Resident fish can save their energy by feeding at cooler times of day. Early mornings and evenings, as well as overcast days, provide the best action. When fishing during the heat of the day, search for shady areas. Shorelines with overhanging trees are usually inhabited by larger predatory fish. Chain pickerel are commonly found lying perfectly still in water as shallow as 6 inches, waiting to ambush passing prey. Crappies and bluegills can be found scanning overhanging branches and protruding weeds, anxiously awaiting for insects to get carelessly close to the waterline.

A damselfly dangles over the waters edge teasing many lurking sunfish family members.

Fly Tackle

Unless you are specifically after small panfish or fishing waters known for trophy-sized largemouth bass or northern pike, the most practical fly rod is a 9-footer for either a 5-weight or 6-weight fly line. Such rods are light enough to provide fun with small, cooperative sunfish, yet have enough backbone to handle startling surprise attacks from brutes lurking out of sight. These rods can easily cast a variety of fly sizes, from tiny nymph patterns to midsize poppers.

Reels, like the fly rods, need not be anything too fancy. If it's panfish you're after, you don't need a football field's length of backing or a high-tech drag, but if you are looking for an all-rounder to aid in fighting that occasional bruiser, a reel with a strong, smooth drag is the best choice. Few pond fish will take extreme amounts of line, let alone show you your backing. Because ponds are shallow and often full of vegetation, a weight-forward floating fly line is best to avoid constantly snagging weeds.

This gorgeous little redear sunfish would be fun on a 3-weight outfit, but be careful, a lunker bass may provide your next strike.

For the most part, choosing a pond fly pattern is not difficult because pond fishes are alert to a wide assortment of foods. I usually start with a small popper. Poppers not only slide snag-free over the tops of weeds, but the popping sound attracts the attention of most warmwater species. If nothing strikes, or if the popper's productivity slows after I catch a few fish, I twitch a beadhead nymph or strip a streamer below the surface. A leech pattern such as a Conehead Woolly Bugger or a baitfish imitation such as the Clouser Deep Minnow will usually reach the bottom, where fish often hide from warm daytime temperatures.

Hazards

For the most part, ponds do not present many dangers, but there are some simple things to be aware of, especially when wading. The often marshy or swampy surroundings of natural ponds can have unstable shorelines. Peat bogs and quicksand can easily end up underfoot. Usually, this leads only to an unexpected fall in shallow muck, but it is possible to get engulfed. If you find yourself stuck, do not struggle. Panicking or aggressive movement leads to sinking deeper. Remain calm and slowly take your last step to stable ground. Usually with little effort it can be reached for an escape.

When wading or float tubing, thick weeds will entangle your feet. Always wear gravel guards, not to keep weeds out, but rather to cover up the shoelace carriers and the knot that keeps your wading shoe tied. These things tend to snag on all kinds of vegetation that brushes by.

Kayaks slide gently over hidden debris in ponds and allow for a stealthy approach on warmwater gamefish.

A good alternative to float tubing is to fish from a kayak or canoe. Both boats maneuver quietly and can pass over debris just inches below the surface. They can go virtually anywhere.

In some regions, ponds are likely places to encounter leeches, snakes, snapping turtles, or in some places, alligators. Be aware of the inhabitants that share your fishing grounds. Never purposely annoy any of these creatures. Waders will protect you from leeches and can help protect against bites by any animal. If there are poisonous snakes in your area, have an evacuation plan. In this day and age, most snakebites are not fatal as long as they receive medical attention immediately. Always expect the best, but plan and be prepared for the worst.

LAKES

Lakes are larger, deeper versions of ponds. They are both natural and artificial, as well. The artificial lakes known as reservoirs or impoundments provide excellent fishing. Although most lakes have some sort of vegetation, it never grows from shoreline to shoreline, because the deepest points do not receive sufficient sunlight to support plant life. Lakes can range from pond size to the size of small oceans. The Great Lakes of North America are so large that the observant angler can see slight tidal changes.

Lakes present many different features. A single lake may have variations in depth contoured by a bottom consisting of bars, humps,

Nothing beats early mornings on one of Minnesota's 10,000 lakes.

and drop-offs. One bay on the same lake may have sand, gravel, and rocks along its bottom, while another may be full of weeds and sunken debris. Reservoirs commonly have submerged standing trees, fence lines, and even old buildings. Shorelines also vary. Beaches, rocky points, bordering forests, river mouths, and springs may all be natural parts of the lakeside. Artificial structures such as power plants, which discharge warm water, boathouses, docks, moored boats, swimming rafts, buoys, and channel markers may also add to the characteristics of a lake.

These varying features provide habitat for all kinds of warmwater fish. Many species of sunfish, such as bluegills, pumpkinseeds, rock bass, smallmouth bass, and largemouth bass prosper, along with closely related species such as yellow, white, and striped bass. You are also likely to find yellow perch, walleyes, sauger, northern pike, muskellunge, tiger muskies, bowfin, freshwater drum, and carp, just to name a few, depending on the region.

Successful anglers are those who know what habitat the targeted species prefer under any given circumstance. For instance, normally, on a crystal-clear northern Minnesota lake, smallmouth bass thrive over a bottom of scattered sunken logs and boulders among gravel and sand in a depth of 6 to 20 feet, an area of abundance for their favorite food, crayfish. In late May and early June on the same lake, however, they will move in as shallow as 2 feet deep to spawn and will remain there for up to two weeks to guard their nests. During fierce storms or unexpected cold snaps, they often become sluggish and retreat and wait out the inclement weather in water as deep as 30 feet.

When unfamiliar with a lake and its species, start by blind casting, covering water and not specific fish. Cover as many areas of the lake possible. Start with casts to obvious structures, such as piers, anchored boats, or a channel marker. Look for sunken trees, large rocks, or vegetated shorelines similar to those of ponds. When fishing in deep water, be sure to try a variety of depths. Start with a surface fly, such as a popper, and end by bouncing the bottom with a crayfish or a weighted minnow pattern on a sinking line.

Many foods appeal to the small-mouth bass, but the crayfish is by far their favorite.

Fly Tackle

Unless the wind is unusually strong or you are seeking large northern pike, muskellunge, or even huge carp, a 9-foot fly rod for a 6-weight line is an excellent all-round choice for lakes. This rod has the strength to handle most freshwater species. It can delicately present a small dry fly to a wary surface-feeding perch and still punch weighted streamers and air-resistant poppers into a stiff wind for tiger muskies or bass.

The big water of lakes often supports a few big fish. A reel with a good drag and capacity for a fair amount of backing is a nice luxury to have. Not only will a strong, smooth drag help slow a lunker retreating to the shelter of a leader-tangling brush pile or boulder field, but it may cushion the tippet-snapping head shake of a toothy walleye. A reel that has the capacity to hold 75 yards of 20-pound backing not only lets you tangle with an occasional common carp, a resident of most lakes, but also gives you that slight edge that you may someday need. Remember, the open range of a lake will allow you to cast long distances, and when you hook up far out, it is possible for even a midsize fish to clear the remaining fly line from the reel and get into your backing.

At least two types of fly line will be necessary, one that floats and one that sinks. A weight-forward floating line will come in handy when fishing top-water, either when casting to cruising, rising fish or when prospecting blindly with poppers. It can also be useful for fishing several feet below the surface by simply weighting the fly and leader. Sinking lines are used to drop flies down to greater depths. They are available in many different forms, from entire sinking lines to a mere 5 feet of sinking tip. Both full-sinking lines and sink-tip lines vary in sink rates from very slow to extremely fast. The slow-sinking lines known as intermediates sink just inches below the surface, while faster-sinking lines offer many sink-rate options, from slow to extra superfast. Another option is a shooting-head system. A collection of shooting heads of various sizes can offer a full range of sink rates and is more affordable than a collection of full fly lines. The more alternatives you carry, the more water you can cover, hence the more fish you can catch.

Twitch a Clouser Deep Minnow attached to a fast sinking fly line through the territory of a smallmouth bass and this is what you'll get.

Flies for lakes, as always, depend on your locale and on the fish you are after. Learn the habits of the fish and always try to match the likely foods available. If catching largemouth bass is my goal in a shallow, lily-pad-covered bay, I fish a weedless floating frog pattern, imitating a major food source for the area. Poppers in general are a good bet. They imitate a variety of struggling baitfish, insects, and small animals and will often quickly entice an explosive strike. If for some reason the top-water action isn't happening, perhaps because of wind, it's time to get down. Streamers that imitate minnows, leeches, and crayfish, or a big, ugly hell-grammite nymph (the larva of a dobsonfly) twitched and stripped slowly along a drop-off will lure a hit from most hungry gamefish.

It won't take long before a largemouth bass finds this frog imitation amongst this incredible habitat.

Hazards

Lake fishing most often means fishing from a boat. Use common sense to match the size and type of boat to the conditions of a specific lake. On large lakes, even the calmest days can turn violently windy in rapidly brewed summer thunderstorms. Be sure that you have the required safety equipment for the lake you are fishing. This will always include life jackets for everyone on board, visual distress signals, a fire extinguisher, a sound-producing device, and proper lights. Always travel with sufficient fuel and a motor that is in perfect working condition, and know the rules of navigation. When traveling in unfamiliar waters, motor slowly. Attentively scan for rocks, boulders, and sunken trees hidden slightly below the surface, as well as for floating debris such as driftwood or logs. It is certainly a good idea to have a radio or cellular phone on board to be able to call for help in an emergency.

Sunset on the Illinois River is prime time to fool a walleye into taking a fly.

RIVERS

Rivers traditionally are associated with fly fishing for trout and other species that thrive in cold, clear waters. But they can be an integral part of the warmwater fly fishing experience, as well. Most fly fishers have one near home. Some rivers are large, some are small, some flow rapidly, while others are slow. Many connect lakes, flow in and out of reservoirs, or fill ponds, while others roll on freely for hundreds of miles. It is inevitable that you will fish them.

Many different forces shape rivers. Current, though, is the main factor, and it flows in many different ways. Fast current is easy to identify: roaring water splashing off rocks, rapids, drifting logs, foam, and other debris distinguish it. Although fast current generally isn't a good place to find warmwater species, this swiftly moving water regularly pours into deep holes where the current slows down, a habitat much more to their liking. Minnows and insects, crayfish, snails, frogs, and mice are swept into these pools because they are unable to swim against the powerful upstream flow of the fast current above them. Since these are foods for warmwater species, you will find them there.

This mouse is safe until he decides to take a dip in his nearby watering hole where chain pickerel, largemouth, and the peculiar bowfin live.

Deep pools frequently exist where a river bends. The outside of the turn will have the majority of the pools, places where the current swirls, creating eddies as it bounces off jammed trees, rock walls, and other rubble. Behind some of these structures are areas without current. These are prime places for large fish to await drifting and passing prey. The bank itself may even be undercut and have overhanging willows or a canopy of leaning trees, creating shade that hides and protects these predators. These are great places to prospect with flies.

The inside of a river bend has the slowest-moving current and is usually shallow and often gravel-bottomed. Although there is less structure here, minnows school in these areas to dodge currents. Predatory fish ordinarily avoid the shallows during a bright, sunny day because they would become easy targets for hungry land predators, but in low-light conditions, especially before sunrise and after sunset, the shallows become worthy places to concentrate fishing efforts. Walleyes are prolific nighttime feeders and are famous for patrolling gravel bars after dark in search of leeches, minnows, and crayfish, but sauger, crappies, rock bass, smallmouth bass, and striped bass are commonly found there when the light is low, as well.

Some rivers, especially if they are deep and slow-moving—the sort of water referred to as bayous in Louisiana and other southern states—will have sloughs or backwaters. These are areas where the river has flooded over its bank and created an area similar to a pond. They are nearly devoid of current, and like a pond, often rich with aquatic plants and other living creatures. As we have already learned, this environment attracts many warmwater species. In northern regions, northern pike, chain pickerel, smallmouth bass, and muskellunge thrive here, but in the bayou, this kind of habitat is a favorite hangout for largemouth bass, rock bass, warmouths, bluegills, crappies, catfish, gar, and carp.

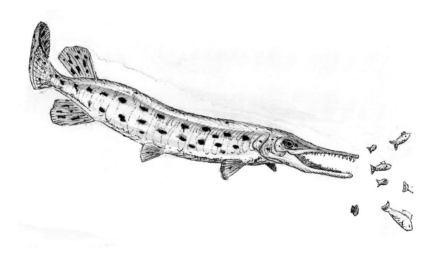

The spotted gar frequently feeds on other fishes and is therefore occasionally taken on flies.

Depending on the region, nearly all warmwater species can be found in rivers. In the Pacific Northwest of the United States, the Columbia River drainage holds enormous walleyes that gorge on the fry of salmon, steelhead, and shad. In the Boundary Waters Canoe Area of Minnesota and the Quetico Provincial Park of Ontario, Canada, smallmouth bass, northern pike, and walleyes compete for food filtered over waterfalls into deep, oxygenated pools. The backwaters of the Saint Lawrence River hold world record muskellunge that camouflage themselves in the dark water, waiting to ambush the unexpecting muskrat or even a small duck. In Alabama, warmouths, redbreast sunfish, bluegills, largemouth bass, gar, pickerel, and many other species enjoy the Mobile-Tensaw Delta, where fresh water turns brackish before feeding the Gulf of Mexico.

A redbreast sunfish from Alabama's Mobile-Tensaw Delta.

Rivers present many new challenges for the fly fisher. Current has a major effect on fly presentation. The fly itself does not sink the way it does in still waters. Moving water pushes a fly along, so that by the time it reaches the desired depth, it may have drifted out of the fishing zone. So in fast current, land your fly well upstream of the desired location, allowing it time to sink. In slower-moving current do not land it as far above, cutting the distance accordingly.

Current also affects the fly line and leader by creating drag. Varied current speeds in the water between the rod tip and the fly tug at the fly line and leader, making it move unnaturally and pulling the fly away from the targeted location. For instance, when casting from a boat in the middle of a river to an inside bend, the current closest to the rod tip is usually moving faster than the current where the fly landed, thus creating a downstream belly in the fly line. As this belly continues to grow, it begins to pull the leader and fly along with it. To prevent this from happening, use a technique known as mending. Mending is simply flipping that downstream belly in the fly line upstream before it begins to pull on the fly and leader and disturbs the drift of the fly.

On rivers, mending often is done repeatedly during every cast, but not always upstream. Sometimes the current across which you cast may be moving more slowly than the current where you land your fly. In this situation, the fly line closest to the rod tip moves more slowly and an upstream belly forms because the fly is drifting faster. In this situation, mend the fly line in the opposite direction, downstream. It is idiosyncrasies like these that make fly fishing a river fun.

Fly Tackle

A good all-round choice for rivers is a 9-foot fly rod for a 5-weight or 6-weight line, but pursuing large warmwater species such as muskellunge in a backwater or striped bass below a dam will require a heavier rod. Current also must be considered. When the current is strong, a seemingly small white bass can pull twice as hard and take twice the line it would on a lake. Not only might a 7-weight rod feel better for the battle, but a reel with a strong drag and a capacity of 75 yards of 20-pound backing might help put your mind at ease and even save a fly line.

Both floating and sinking fly lines will be necessary. The floating line is ideal when searching shallow inside turns and for fishing poppers far back in weedy sloughs. Intermediate to fast-sinking sink-tip and full-sinking lines will help submerge flies, cutting through current to the bottom of deep holes, where fish reside.

Although most warmwater species will take advantage of a floating meal such as a large insect or a small swimming frog, subsurface flies consistently produce strikes. Cast streamer patterns that will move some water and get the attention of fish. Cast toward structured banks and don't miss unusually deep inside turns. Use various stripping speeds near the surface with lightly weighted patterns first, then gradually drop down in depth with heavier patterns. Once you start getting strikes on a regular basis, stick to that depth, fly choice, and stripping method. Heavily weighted Clouser Deep Minnows and conehead patterns are great for creating a jiglike action that entices any warmwater species, as well as prowling trout.

Hazards

A common method of fishing a river is to drift downstream in a boat with oars. While one person controls the drift by steering and rowing against the current, another casts. The rower must be constantly alert, looking downstream for increases in current and obstacles such as rocks, trees, overhanging willows, and logs. When these obstacles protrude, they are easy to avoid because they are obvious from a distance. Face directly toward them, row against the current, and steer away from these potential dangers well in advance.

Sleepers, however, are the most common cause of boat accidents on a river. Sleepers are the same obstacles concealed just below the surface, making them difficult to recognize until it is sometimes too late. Boaters frequently get hung up on them or even capsized. Watch for any unusual disturbances in the river's surface. Sleepers hide where the current swishes and boils in a mysterious manner.

Some large rivers are navigable by motorboat. Unless you are extremely familiar with such a river, avoid fast speeds. Currents in large rivers are constantly relocating logs, driftwood, and other debris, making it difficult to guarantee a clear path at any time. Always remain alert for protruding obstacles, sleepers, and drifting debris, as well as other boat traffic.

Oregon's John Day River is an excellent smallmouth fishery, but it takes a good oarsman to lead a safe trip.

Wading is the most common method of fly fishing a river. Always be aware of swiftly moving currents, drop-offs, and unstable bottoms. Watch every step you take to avoid tripping over or entangling in debris such as tree branches, brush piles, weeds, or a loose rock. When wearing waders, always wear a tightly secured wading belt. If you fish frequently, regardless of how careful you are, expect an occasional unwanted swim. The wading belt will prevent water from gushing in and filling your waders, which could result in drowning. Felt soles on wading shoes and the use of a wading staff also can be beneficial when walking on slippery rocks.

CANALS

Canals are artificial waterways used for navigation, flood control, irrigation, and to replenish reservoirs for human use. Because they can connect any of the previous three water types, they are home to many warmwater species.

Canals range anywhere from a few feet to several hundred feet across. Some are short, connecting two nearby bodies of water, while others, such as the Panama Canal, are over one hundred miles long. Some have swift current, like many rivers, while others appear almost

Venturing off Massachusetts's Ipswich River into a canal can provide hours of action for chain pickerel.

stagnant. Although artificial, canals have many features that attract fish both big and small. Seawalls, bridges, culverts, spillways, shoreline vegetation, and riprap all provide nooks and crannies that create shelter for warmwater species.

Florida has perhaps the most sophisticated canal system in the United States. Located in a prime hurricane and tropical-storm region, Florida's canals have poured torrential rains back to cypress swamps, bayous, lakes, and the ocean repeatedly since their construction in the early 1900s. Today, these canals do more than drain water. Many flow through highly urbanized areas and are frequently used by boaters. They are also commonly fished. Largemouth bass, bluegills, crappies, and chain pickerel, as well as tarpon and snook, which can tolerate fresh water, once dominated such places, but the illegal release of over twenty-five exotic species by owners of home aquariums who think it is the humane thing to do with unwanted pet fish poses a threat to these natives.

Among these exotic species, the cichlid family, fierce predators that are native to the rivers and lakes of Africa and Central and South America, have taken over in many places. Several types of tilapia, oscar, and guapote are now found. Cichlids breed rapidly and compete with indigenous species for food and spawning locations. Although these and other exotics cannot extend their range far northward in Florida because of their inability to tolerate low water temperatures, many South Florida canals are infested with these fish.

The colorful butterfly peacock bass will attack a fly with vengeance.

In 1984, the butterfly peacock bass, a native of South America, was legally introduced to help control the abundant undesirable exotics. Well over a decade later, it has been proven that these hearty eating machines have helped do so. Not only that, but the peacocks have also attracted the attention of many anglers. The colorful bass is an aggressive cichlid itself and will attack both noisy top-water and subsurface flies as commendably as any North American gamefish.

As in a river, in a canal you must identify places that will likely hold fish. First, note the speed of the current. Although uncommon, fast currents do occur in canals, particularly after a heavy rain. As we have already learned, most species of warmwater fish prefer to hold in slower, deeper pools in moving water. This presents an immediate challenge because unlike rivers, canals tend to be uniform in depth all the way through, and deep holes may not exist. Search out obstructions such as a cement bridge piling, fallen tree, riprap, or even submerged pipe.

One of my favorite locations is where canals intersect. Here you often find a seam formed by the different speeds of current. This is an ideal spot to find holding fish. Angle a cast slightly upstream into the slower-moving current and let your fly drift and swing downstream toward the seam. Just before it gets there, begin your retrieve. A fly that sinks fast and provides jigging action is best. I like to bounce the bottom with a conehead or a Clouser Deep Minnow with the biggest eyes my casting can handle. Big eyes provide maximum weight, taking the fly to the bottom quickly. After thoroughly covering the confluence of the two canals, fish your way up the slower of the two. You should find a concentration of fish that have retreated from the faster currents from below. Often, the joining canal will lead to a dead end for another great place to make some persistent casts. Dead ends usually have little or no current, something warmwater species enjoy, as well as lots of overhanging vegetation for cover.

Fly Tackle

Considering the fact that big bass, pickerel, and where canals are plentiful, various cichlids may take your fly, a 9-foot rod for either a 6-weight or a 7-weight line is perfect. However, if you are specifically panfishing, then drop down to a 4-weight and have some fun. Purchase a reel to match your fishing situation, as well. A reel with a smooth drag and capacity for 50 yards of 20-pound backing will be more than enough.

No Florida Cichlid is going to eat this hefty largemouth bass.

Give yourself extra versatility for covering the different types of water in a canal. Keep both a weight-forward floating and a sinking fly line handy at all times. Although poppers are always a good choice for chasing warmwater species, in canals, have plenty of Clouser Deep Minnows, coneheads, and other small fish and leech imitations available.

Hazards

Because canals are artificial, water flows are sometimes regulated. You must beware of rising levels and increases in currents while wading or boating. Never enter the water close to the headgates that control water flows, or close to diversion dams, culverts, or in large canals, locks. As in any boating situation, watch for other traffic. Canals are often narrow. Stopping to cast in the middle of a travel route is very dangerous.

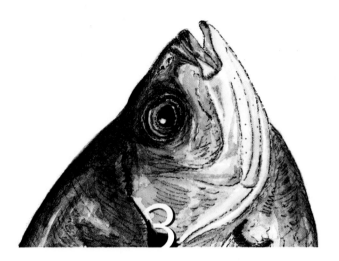

FLIES AND EQUIPMENT

The cost of a top-quality fly-fishing outfit often scares the potential warmwater fly fisher away from trying the sport. But if you have fly-fishing equipment for trout, you may already have what you need to get started in the warmwater branch of the sport. Naturally, I'm not recommending chasing tiger muskies with a 4-weight or 5-weight rod, but for many of the warmwater species, you're in business with gear like that. Use your light rod for panfish, do your best with what you have, and wait to buy a heavier warmwater outfit, if you need one, after you have learned more about the kinds of warmwater fly fishing that you will do most of the time.

Tackle choices abound for the warmwater flyrodder. You can start with a combination outfit containing a rod, reel, and line for between $199 and $395. Or you can piece together a luxurious outfit yourself with an exquisitely engineered reel and match it to a graphite rod crafted to the finest standards of finish and performance.

Remember, despite its substantial cost, modern equipment is an excellent value, and most is guaranteed for life. You are making a worthwhile investment that will provide great satisfaction during frequent trips to your favorite fishing holes.

Another legitimate concern is the complicated nature of fly-fishing equipment. Chapter 2 provided some general equipment recommendations for various types of water. Now we'll examine the specifics of equipment selection. Gear selection can be simpler than you think.

RODS

If you already fly fish, then you are ready for warmwater fishing because you have a fly rod. I've seen largemouth bass landed on 2-weights and northern pike landed on 4-weights. But as a practical matter, these rods are too light for many conditions encountered in warmwater fly fishing. The ideal arsenal would consist of a 9-foot rod for a 3-weight or 4-weight line, a 9-foot 6-weight or 7-weight, and a 9-foot or 9 1/2-foot 8-weight or 9-weight. Since this would likely be too costly for the first warmwater venture for most anglers, pick the weight that is best for the size and species of fish you are most likely to encounter.

A 3-weight or 4-weight rod may be a bit light for many situations in warmwater, but one of these rods can be a blast when conditions allow for its use. Imagine a day at a local pond with almost no wind and bluegills, crappies, and other panfish surfacing everywhere. With a 7-weight, a rod hefty enough to use for bass, your fly line would land with such impact that almost every panfish would spook. With a 3-weight or 4-weight, the presentation is softer and more likely to reward you with a hookup, an exciting struggle, and a thrill as you land a 12-inch crappie.

This beautiful black crappie was plucking insects off the lily pads before falling for a small standard popper.

A 6-weight, though, is the universal weight for warmwater fly fishing. It provides enough power to land anything from a fairly big largemouth to a small northern pike while still being light enough to provide great fun fighting a bluegill or other panfish. I never leave the dock or car without my 6-weight, even when I'm specifically targeting large fish. My favorite 6-weight is 9 feet long. Although 8 1/2-foot rods are common and will do the job, the extra 6 inches come in handy for lifting a back cast above obstructions behind me while beach fishing. The taller rod also hoists the fly line over snags while fighting a fish in a debris-filled bay or pond.

Unless you are seeking big warmwater species such as trophy largemouths, striped bass, northern pike, muskellunge, tiger muskies, or even carp, these light and medium rods will be more than adequate. Such larger species, however, require a larger rod.

I recommend an 8-weight or 9-weight. If at present your heaviest fly rod is a 6-weight, then go with the 8-weight. If you already have a 7-weight, skip the 8-weight and go to the 9-weight. My theory is that if your going to have a limited number of rods, say three, you should spread them out a bit. A 4-weight, a 6-weight, and an 8-weight makes a great collection. So does a 5-weight, 7-weight, and 9-weight, and it accomplishes nearly the same tasks. If you're like me, you will eventually fill in the gaps later.

Whether you choose an 8-weight or a 9-weight, it will be a nice addition to your artillery. Each of these fly rods has the additional backbone needed to turn a colossal carp on a grassy flat or lift a gigantic muskellunge from the depths straight beneath the boat on a choppy lake. They can also heave the flies often needed to get the attention of these fellows. Imagine trying to throw an 8-inch streamer pattern attached to 12 inches of wire on a windy day to tiger muskie with a light rod. It would be downright dangerous for most of the people that I know.

On these heavy rods, additional length is also an option. In both fresh and salt water, 9 1/2 feet is a popular length for both 8-weights and 9-weights. If I had it my way, I would have both. Here again, the extra 6 inches is good for lifting a fly line over obstacles.

Monster stripers such as this 30-pounder require at least a 9-weight!

This is especially handy when yanking on a large northern pike as he zips back and forth in a foot of water among logs, roots, reeds, cattails, and other protruding plants. However, what is gained by the added length sometimes can be just as quickly lost. That same length lessens the lifting power needed when a stubborn monster gets down deep below the boat, which often leads to a lengthened battle and can result in the loss of a big fish.

REELS

A trout reel rarely does more than store line, although strong drags and expanded backing capacities usually are available. For panfish, that same simple trout reel is ideal. But when you begin to pursue some of the more robust members of the warmwater family, you must upgrade the requirements. At a minimum, a big-fish reel should have a smooth drag and be able to endure repeated explosive runs. It also should be able to hold at least 75 yards of backing.

Both direct-drive and multiplier reels are suited to warmwater fly fishing. The direct-drive reel collects line at a 1:1 retrieve ratio. That is, every turn of the reel handle rotates the spool once. The multiplier uses gears to collect line at a ratio of approximately 2 1/2 to 1, which makes for faster retrieves. That sounds appealing, especially considering the long runs a carp or striped bass can make, but multipliers have many more parts, and thus more things that can fail. With the recent introduction of large-arbor direct-drive reels that have a large circumference and collect line rapidly anyway, I recommend sticking with direct-drive.

Direct-drive reels are available in many sizes, shapes, and drag efficiencies. The most important issue here is the drag. Although little or no drag is necessary on reels used for panfish, a reel with a strong, smooth drag is an advantage when battling hard-fighting fish. Such a reel costs more than a reel with little or no drag, however. If you want to save some money, purchase a reel with the most primitive of drags: a dual-pawl or single-pawl system. A pawl is basically a triangular piece of metal, graphite, or plastic that is pushed by a spring against the teeth of the spool, thus creating a minimal amount of resistance. Generally, all it does is create enough pressure to prevent a backlash when you strip line off the reel to begin fishing. It may sound cheap, but for small fish, it works just fine.

I have caught large fish on reels with pawl drag systems. As every angler knows, where there are small fish, there are big fish, and every once in awhile you will hook into one on light tackle. These days, most reels have an option called rim control. The outer rim of the reel's spool sticks out slightly past the frame of the reel, so that as it spins while a fish takes line, you can put a finger or a thumb against it. Essentially, you become your own drag. If you're skillful at it and let the spool spin against your thumb smoothly, you'll have a good chance of slowing down and landing a fish the size of King Kong. The reel you decide on definitely should have rim control.

For most panfish, a dual-pawl system fly reel attached to a 3-weight rod works excellent, but when you run into hog bluegills such as this one, you might need to step up your outfit a notch.

Most reels also provide backing capacity whether you need it or not, so when you need it, it's there. Backing also serves several purposes beyond allowing fish to take out more line. It helps the reel perform better by adding to the diameter of the spool, thus improving retrieve speeds. It also reduces the coiling of the fly line after it has been spooled for a while. In addition, its weight helps balance out the overall outfit of fly rod, line, and reel.

If you intend to match a reel to the lightweight fly rod we talked about, say a 4-weight, then you should purchase a basic reel of the sort just described. For a medium-weight fly rod, a 5-weight, 6-weight, or perhaps a 7-weight, I would consider investing some extra money and getting a reel with a disc drag. A knob, usually on the back of the reel, pushes a disc inside, ordinarily a material such as Teflon or cork, against the reel spool as the knob is tightened. The surface area of this disc slows the turning reel spool, thus causing a fish tugging away to work harder and begin to tire.

A major concern here is drag smoothness. A drag that flutters or jerks can be a problem. Fluttering and jerking occur when the drag sticks and releases as line is pulled off the reel. This can break off a worthy fish. With a smooth drag, the line leaves the reel at a consistent pace, making it nearly impossible for a fish to break off. It is always a good idea to test the drags on your reels before a trip. Use a fishing scale to set the drag. Even with the most expensive and sophisticated reels, you will only need three to four pounds of pressure.

When matching a reel for your heavy 8-weight or 9-weight outfit, always invest in a strong, smooth drag. Whether you're after northern pike the length of small trees, shad-stuffed striped bass, or bullying carp, if you want to catch these hogs with any regularity, pair up your big stick with the highest-quality reel you can afford.

Make sure this reel has enough backing capacity. For your heavy outfit, a minimum of 75 yards of 20-pound backing is required. In fact, a striped bass or huge carp hooked below a tailwater could head for fast current and easily peal off over a hundred yards in a hurry. The bottom line is simple. Big fish require a big reel.

Purchasing an extra spool for your reel should always be a consideration. It may seem to be just one more expense at first, but the convenience of being able to switch from a floating line to a sinking line in a matter of seconds is worth it. For several of my reels, I own as many as four extra spools, giving me a choice of four fly lines at all times. They take up little space in my tackle bag, and I can switch them in a matter of seconds.

BACKING

Backing is the first line that goes on a fly reel's spool. The two most commonly used materials are either 20-pound test Dacron or Micron. Both stretch very little and lie smoothly on the spool. They resist mildew and rot, and they dry quickly. The amount of backing depends on the fish you are pursuing. For most warmwater species, backing is not a concern, so just load the reel with the recommended amount to balance your outfit. For the largest members of the warmwater fishes, you will likely be using a heavy 8-weight or 9-weight outfit. Chances are that the compatible reel will call for at least 150 yards of backing, the maximum amount necessary for nearly all warmwater species.

FLY LINE

Although there are many different fly-line tapers, there are only two types used for warmwater fly fishing: weight-forward (WF) and shooting tapers (ST). Both are designed to make quick and long casts and to help carry the large, air-resistant flies that are often used for warmwater species.

"Weight-forward" means that the majority of the line's casting weight is located in the first 30 feet of line, in a section that tapers down to a tip that facilitates delicate presentations or helps turn over big flies, depending on the line. The remainder of the line is a thinner running line, designed to slide easily through the rod guides. Weight-forward lines range anywhere from 82 to 105 feet in total length.

Weight-forward lines are further divided into specialty lines such as rocket tapers, bass tapers, bass-bug tapers, pike/musky tapers, pike lines, warmwater fly lines, and tropic plus lines. Each of these varies in total length and in the amount and distribution of the weight concentrated in the forward part of the line.

As you can tell by the names, some of these specialty lines are formulated for warmwater fly fishing. The bass taper has a specially calculated short front taper and a relatively short weight-forward body section, which together provide a more effective turnover of large, air-resistant flies during the cast. The pike/musky taper has an even shorter front taper and body that helps deliver the feather-duster-sized flies that commonly are used for these fish. Many of these lines are also designed with medium-stiff cores. Originally designed to keep lines from softening and wilting under the broiling tropical sun in saltwater fly-fishing locations, these cores are now used in lines intended for the hottest freshwater climates, as well.

When fishing a shallow lake or pond a weight-forward floating fly line will be best.

So far, we have discussed only floating lines. There are numerous options among sinking lines, as well. Full-sinking lines that submerge slowly, such as the intermediate, "clear camo" (which is designed to become invisible in the water), and stillwater lines retrieve flies slightly under the surface, while the various steady-sinking, sinking rocket taper, wet-cel, and uniform-sinking graduated-density lines drop flies to a wide range of depths. Each of the faster-sinking lines is available in different sink rates, from fast to extra superfast.

Sink-tip lines are hybrids—the tip sinks and the running line floats. Although they are the most difficult kind of line to cast, they are very popular. Sink-tip lines with tips from 5 to 24 feet long are available in many different sink rates.

Because most warmwater species are found in less than 20 feet of water, and because many will smash a noisy top-water popper, I would suggest purchasing a floating line first. Sinking lines are excellent for fishing flies down deep, but a floating line attached to a long leader and a weighted fly can reach commonly fished depths, as well. Ideally, you should have both floating and sinking lines rigged on a pair of rods.

For blind casting, it is helpful to make long casts that explore a variety of depths. This is when shooting heads (also called shooting tapers) come into their own. A shooting head is a section of weight-forward fly line 30 feet long or slightly shorter that is attached by a loop-to-loop system (illustrated in the knot section of the next chapter) to the end of a running line. The running line can be thin, level fly line, 25-pound to 35-pound mono, or braided mono. The small diameter of the running line creates little friction while traveling through a fly rod's guides. This allows for long casts.

Shooting tapers, like weight-forward fly lines, come in both floating and sinking versions, and in many sink rates. Most sinking shooting tapers are measured in grains. A 150-grain shooting taper, which typically is used on a 5-weight rod, is light and sinks at a slower rate than a heavy, 250-grain taper used on a 9-weight rod. Shooting tapers are not nearly as expensive as entire fly lines. A shooting-taper system allows you to carry a variety of lines to attain a variety of depths. If you are really ambitious, you can make your own heads by cutting old full-length floating or sinking fly lines to the desired length.

FLIES

The flies you'll need will vary depending on the warmwater fish you're after and the environment in which they live. It is always best to use a fly that imitates the predominant natural food source. Knowing what this is may be challenging, because food sources change with seasons and weather patterns. In Chapters 7 and 8, I list my favorite flies for a variety of warmwater species, and in Appendix B, I include color photos of each fly. You will notice that a lot of the same patterns are listed for many different species of fish, making your first warmwater fly collection much easier to build than you may have thought possible.

ADDITIONAL EQUIPMENT

There are several additional items that can be useful during your warmwater fly-fishing experience. The first few are mandatory, no matter where you go or when you go. Never go anywhere without sufficient rain gear. Have tops and bottoms, even when fishing in tropical regions. A hat and polarized sunglasses also are mandatory to protect you from the sun and to remove glare from the water, allowing your vision to penetrate the surface. Always throw some sunscreen and insect repellent into your kit, and take plenty of drinking water to help prevent dehydration.

Other items that you should not be without are a good pair of pliers that can remove a hook as well as smash down a barb and cut wire and heavy mono, a hook hone, and spare leaders and leader materials. Where you fish will determine whether you need hip boots or waders, a flashlight, dry-fly floatant, dry-fly powder, split shot, a vest or fanny pack, and extra fly boxes.

A good pair of pliers are essential when removing a fly from toothy critters like the northern pike.

This youngster wouldn't have caught this hearty smallmouth bass if it weren't for good knots.

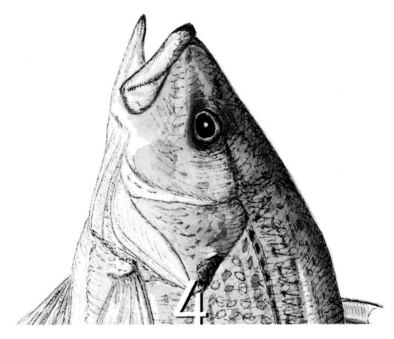

KNOTS

Knots have always been difficult for most anglers. However, knots keep you connected to fish, so you need to tie them to perfection. A variety of knots accomplish the same purpose. With the exception of the Spider Hitch and the Bimini Twist, I have kept things simple, illustrating only one specific knot for each key point in your system, beginning with the attachment of the backing to the reel and working out to the attachment of the fly to the leader. The key points in between are the connection of the fly line to the backing, the leader butt to fly line, the tippet to leader, and in special leaders that have a shock tippet or bite tippet, the connection of the shock tippet to the tippet. With a little practice, you can master these knots. When you can tie them well, your overall fishing will improve.

ATTACHING THE BACKING TO THE REEL

First you must attach the backing to the fly reel's spool arbor. A good knot is important here, because if this knot were to break, you would lose the fly, leader, line, and backing. I prefer to lose just the fly. The Arbor Knot is excellent for this first link.

Arbor Knot

Step 1. Tie several Overhand Knots in the tag end of the backing.
Wrap the backing around the spool arbor several times.
Tie an Overhand Knot around the standing line and secure it.
Pull on the standing line until the knots meet tightly against
the spool arbor.

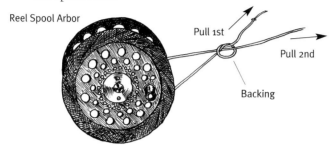

PREPARING THE BACKING TO ATTACH TO THE FLY LINE

There are probably more arguments about the best knot for attaching the backing to fly line than there are about how to connect any other elements of the fly-fishing system. Some feel that having a small, smooth knot that slides through the rod guides easily is more important than the strength of the knot itself, while others go for strength and worry about the smoothness later. Personally, I go for both. I use a loop-to-loop connection that has proven itself to me against some of the world's toughest, speediest, backing-stealing fish. You might ask, "If it's that strong, isn't it overkill for panfish?" Sure, but the way I look at it, the day a bluegill takes me to my backing is the day I want the strongest backing-to-fly-line knot possible. Of course, this will never happen, and that's really my point. When this knot is involved in battle, it needs to be strong, and when it's not, it will be buried under fly line.

When each loop is tied properly, the loop-to-loop connection is one of the strongest links possible. This is also by far the fastest way to make any connection. Therefore, I use loops for many parts of my fly-fishing system. To construct the loop-to-loop connection where the backing meets the fly line, I make a loop in my backing with a Spider Hitch and a loop on the back end of my fly line by making a Whipped Loop.

I am often asked, "Is the Spider Hitch as strong as the Bimini Twist?" No, the Bimini Twist has 100 percent knot strength, while the Spider Hitch has about 98 percent. Technically, this means that the

Spider Hitch will break twice every hundred tries, while the Bimini will not. After carefully testing the Spider Hitch on scales and after years of on-the-water use, I still rate it as an excellent knot and a good choice for the beginner. It is easy to learn and takes less than 10 seconds to tie.

The Bimini Twist, on the other hand, is difficult to learn and takes nearly a minute to tie. However, its proven strength makes it a worthy knot to learn. Either of these two excellent, but different knots can be used to construct a loop in the backing to receive the fly line. You decide for yourself which knot suits you best.

Spider Hitch

Step 1. Make a large loop 25 to 30 inches in length out of the tag end of the backing. Near the base of this loop, make a small reverse loop and pinch it between your thumb and forefinger.

Step 2. Be sure that your thumb extends past your forefinger and that the small loop extends past your thumb.

Step 3. Wind the double line from the large loop around both your thumb and the small loop six to eight times and pass the remainder of the large loop through the smaller loop.

Step 4. Now pull evenly to make the turns unwind off the thumb. Tighten. The finished loop should be large enough to allow you to pass a line on a manufacturer's spool through it.

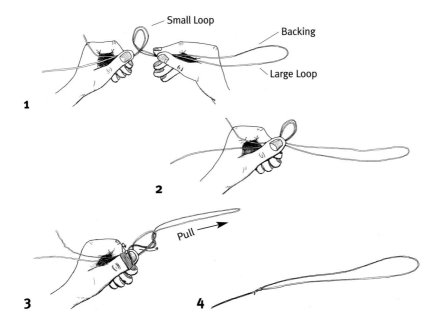

Bimini Twist

Step 1. Make a large loop 30 to 40 inches in length out of the tag end of the backing and twist the loop 21 times.

Step 2. Insert both feet inside the tightly wound loop. While holding firmly on the standing line, pull tight with the tag end slightly downward and away.

Step 3. This creates tension, and as you continue to pull the tag end downward, a second set of tight winds will form over the top of the first and automatically roll their way down to the apex of the loop. Do not let up on the tension.

Step 4. Using a simple Half Hitch, lock the winds in place around each leg of the loop individually.

Step 5. Do a Half Hitch around both legs of the loop together.

Step 6. Secure with a Triple Half Hitch around both legs of the loop together. Pull tight and trim.

Step 7. With the tension taken away, the finished knot will twist. This is the way it is supposed to be. Rub in a coat of a glue that is pliable when it dries, such as Pliobond or Aquaseal, onto the knot itself and allow it to cure. The finished loop should be large enough to allow you to pass a line on a manufacturer's spool through it.

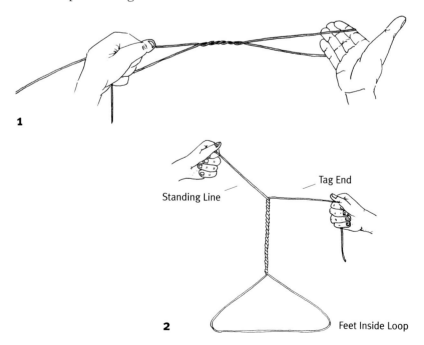

1

Standing Line

Tag End

2

Feet Inside Loop

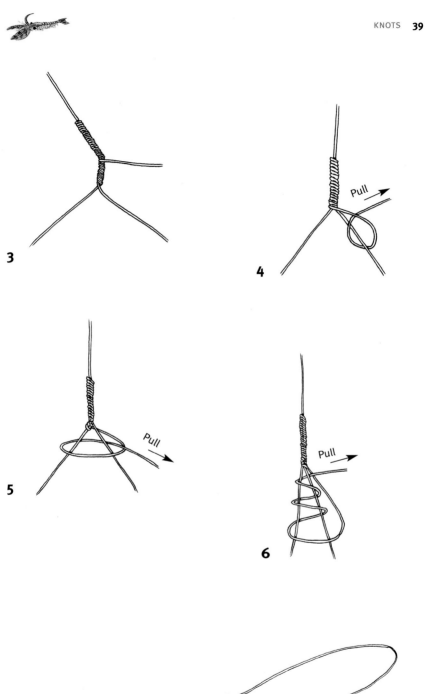

3

4

Pull

5

Pull

6

Pull

7

Spider Hitch or Bimini Twist Loop with a Surgeon's Knot

I strengthen the loop in the backing even further by creating a double-line loop. This is done by making a Surgeon's Knot in the loop.

Step 1. Double back the end of the loop against itself.

Step 2. Tie an Overhand Knot using the loop.

Step 3. Make another pass through the newly created loop, making it a Double Overhand Knot.

Step 4. Pull tight.

Under great pulling forces, the double line is stronger than a single line and is also less likely to cut through the opposing loop with which it is linked.

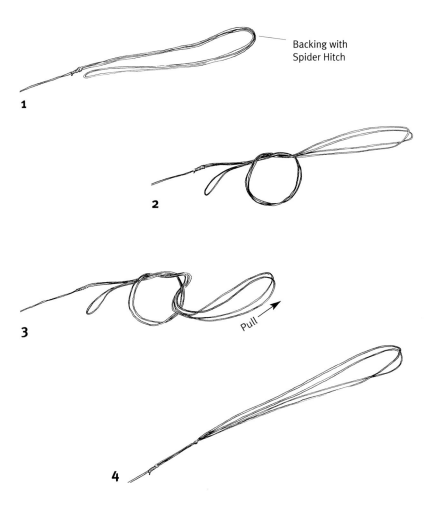

Backing with
Spider Hitch

1

2

3

Pull

4

ATTACHING THE FLY LINE TO THE BACKING AND THE LEADER

To attach the fly line to the backing—and to attach the leader to the other end of the line—I construct a whipped loop out of the fly line itself. It takes nearly two minutes to whip a loop, but this is a strong knot.

Whipping a Loop

Step 1. Trim the tag end of the fly line at an angle as if creating a point. Fold it over to form a small loop approximately an inch in length.

Step 2. Load a fly-tying bobbin with 3/0 or larger thread, but wrap the thread four times around the bobbin leg before threading. Hold the tag end of the thread against the looped fly line. Swing the bobbin hard, burying the thread into the finish of the fly line and binding the tag end of the fly line to the standing end.

Step 3. After you have a smooth connection, tie the thread off with several Half Hitches. Coat the finished loop with a pliable glue such as Pliobond or Aquaseal and allow it to cure.

Repeat this procedure at the front end of the fly line. You now are ready to connect the fly line to the backing and install a leader.

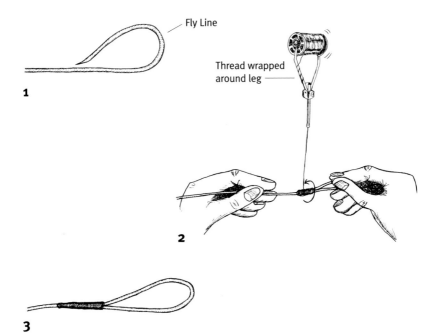

Fly Line

Thread wrapped around leg

1

2

3

JOINING THE LOOPS

In order for any loop-to-loop connection to maintain its maximum strength, it must be linked correctly.

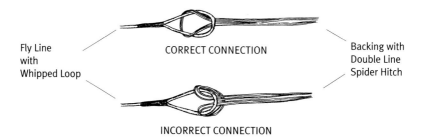

Fly Line
with
Whipped Loop

CORRECT CONNECTION

Backing with
Double Line
Spider Hitch

INCORRECT CONNECTION

LEADERS AND THE REST OF THE KNOTS

Long, supple leaders—the choice of trout anglers—are not a good choice for warmwater fly fishing. Short leaders with thick butts and stronger than normal tippets are necessary for turning over large flies. These beefier leaders also help protect against abrasion, which is frequently a problem when fighting warmwater adversaries.

I will discuss three different types of leaders throughout the remainder of the book: Type A (Basic Leader), Type B (Custom Class and Shock Tippet Leader), and Type C (Toothy-Critter Leader).

Type A Leader

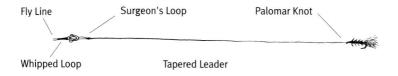

Fly Line

Surgeon's Loop

Palomar Knot

Whipped Loop

Tapered Leader

A Type A leader is the simplest, and resembles a normal trout leader, but is heavier. It is the only leader that I would recommend purchasing premade. It is basically a knotless tapered leader of a specific length and a specific tippet strength. It is used for most of the warmwater species such as the sunfishes that do not have tippet-cutting sharp teeth or abrasive gill plates or skin.

You need to learn three new knots when using a store-bought, premade Type A leader. The Surgeon's Loop, for attaching the leader to the Whipped Loop on the end of the fly line, the Palomar Knot, for tying the fly snug to the tippet (the fine end of the leader), and the Non-slip Mono Loop, a loop knot that allows for more action when tying a popper to the tippet. Here is how you tie them.

Surgeon's Loop

A Surgeon's Loop is the easiest leader loop to tie. We've already discussed the basic technique in using a Surgeon's Knot to strengthen a Spider Hitch or Bimini Twist Loop. The Surgeon's Loop allows quick leader changes, and it is strong.

Step 1. Double back the tag end of the leader butt against the standing line and form a loop approximately six inches long. Tie an Overhand Knot using the loop, but don't pull tight.

Step 2. Make another pass with the first loop through the opening of the newly created loop, forming a Double Overhand Knot.

Step 3. Pull tight.

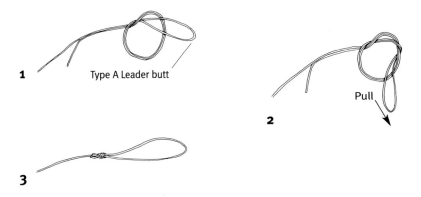

Palomar Knot

Although the Palomar Knot uses up more tippet than most knots, it is exceptionally strong and a simple way to tie the tippet to the fly.

Step 1. Make a loop at least 4 inches long at the end of your tippet. Pass the loop through the eye of the fly.

Step 2. Tie an Overhand Knot with the loop around the standing end and the leader tag end.

Step 3. Pass the fly through the loop and pull the leader gently until it completely clears the fly.

Step 4. Continue to pull the tag end and standing line while holding the fly firmly until the knot is snug.

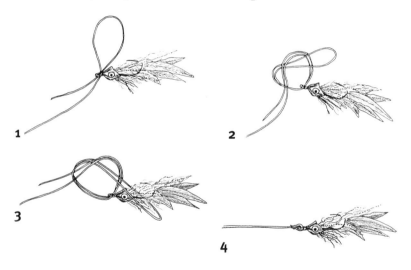

Non-Slip Mono Loop

A fly tightly knotted to a tippet has less swimming action than a fly that is allowed to swing freely in a loop. It is especially important that you use this knot when fishing poppers to get the proper popping action or when using especially heavy tippet material such as mono shock tippets, which we will learn about when discussing Type B leaders.

Step 1. Before attaching the fly, make an Overhand Loop in your tippet material 3 inches back from the tag end to which the fly will be attached.

Step 2. Run the tag end through the eye of the fly and up through the Overhand Loop, entering the loop on the same side the tag end exited.

Step 3. Wrap the tag end around the standing line three to four turns and insert the tag back through the Overhand Loop (heavier tippet material requires fewer turns).

Step 4. Moisten the knot and work into place by pulling lightly on the leader tag end and pulling harder on the hook.

A loop knot is the best choice when fishing poppers. This longeared sunfish couldn't resist.

Replacing Worn Tippet

The tippet section of a leader requires frequent replacement. When a premade Type A leader is taken out of the package, it is ready to go. The tippet section is already built in, but every time you change flies, a few inches are lost, until finally the tippet section is altogether gone. At this time, not only are you fishing with a leader that is shorter than you need, but you begin tying flies to a much thicker, stronger part of the leader. Often, this is so thick and strong that it will hinder the action of your fly and even be noticeable to the fish, thus reducing the chance of strikes.

Wear and tear from tough battles also can lead to the need to change tippets. After I wrestle a scrappy largemouth bass from a brush pile, or after even a short battle with a toothy chain pickerel that stole my fly from a crappie, I make it a point to change the tippet section of my leader.

Typically, the amount of replacement tippet needed is about two feet. However, I often add about thirty inches, giving me an extra few fly changes from the start.

Surgeon's Knot

The Surgeon's Knot is also a strong, simple knot used for joining two lines of equal or unequal diameters, and therefore it is ideal for attaching replacement tippet. The basic technique remains the same as we already have discussed. The situation and materials, though, are a little bit different.

Step 1. Lay 4 inches of the tippet against 4 inches of the remaining end of leader and make an Overhand Knot, drawing the loose end of the tippet through the loop thus formed. Do not pull tight.

Step 2. Make another Overhand Knot, pulling the entire tippet through a second time, creating a Double Overhand Knot.

Step 3. Pull tight by holding the tag end of the tippet against the standing end of the leader in one hand and the tag end of the leader and the standing tippet in the other.

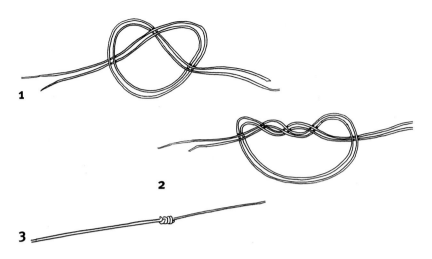

1

2

3

Unfortunately, the Type A leader is not the best choice for all warmwater species. Some of these fish have sharp teeth that can easily wear through even a 20-pound tippet during battle. Therefore, Type B leaders are necessary.

Type B Leader

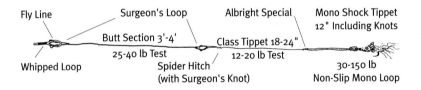

Fly Line	Surgeon's Loop	Albright Special	Mono Shock Tippet 12" Including Knots
	Butt Section 3'-4'	Class Tippet 18-24"	
	25-40 lb Test	12-20 lb Test	
Whipped Loop	Spider Hitch (with Surgeon's Knot)		30-150 lb Non-Slip Mono Loop

Learn to build the Type B leader yourself, and do not purchase it premade. It consists of three separate sections—the butt, class tippet, and shock tippet. The shock tippet is the last section and is made from a heavy piece of mono no more than 12 inches long. Substituting a wire bite tippet for the mono produces what I'm calling a Type C leader.

The Type B leader is for species that are too smart to eat a fly attached to wire. Educated northern pike, muskellunge, and tiger muskies that may have been caught and released a time or two, as well as exotics such as the guapote, peacock bass, and freshwater dorado, require the harder-to-see heavy mono shock tippet. Its strength can range anywhere from 30-pound to 150-pound test. The larger your quarry, the heavier the shock tippet may be.

The exotic guapote of Costa Rica's Lake Arenal has strong jaws well equipped with sharp teeth and requires the use of shock tippet.

The class tippet is the section between the leader butt and the shock tippet and is made of weaker material than the shock tippet. Anglers often ask, "If a fish will eat the fly while attached to the heavy shock tippet, why even have a light class tippet section in the middle?" The answer is that a leader must have a section that is of a weaker material than the backing and fly line to prevent the loss of an entire fly line.

The butt section of the leader is a piece of 30-pound to 40-pound-test mono that not only adds 3 to 4 feet of needed length to the leader to separate fly line from the fly, but also helps turn over a leader with a bulky warmwater fly and shock tippet.

The butt section and the class tippet are looped together using different knots. The butt section has a Surgeon's Loop, while the class tippet has a Spider Hitch with a Surgeon's Knot in it, thus creating a double line.

One new knot is necessary for attaching a mono shock tippet to a class tippet —the Albright Special.

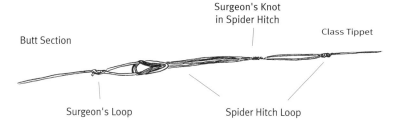

Surgeon's Knot
in Spider Hitch

Class Tippet

Butt Section

Surgeon's Loop

Spider Hitch Loop

Albright Special Knot

Step 1. Tie a loop in the end of the class tippet with either a Spider Hitch or a Bimini Twist to attach the shock tippet. Create a tight bend in the end of the mono shock tippet that will attach to the class tippet. Push the loop of the class tippet through the shock tippet's bend. Keeping the bend in the mono shock tippet, hold the loop from the class tippet firmly between your thumb and forefinger.

Step 2. With the class tippet loop, make 10 wraps toward the bend in the shock tippet and push the end of the class tippet loop back through the shock tippet bend in the opposite direction from the point where it originally entered.

Step 3. Pull gently to tighten the wraps around the shock tippet bend and carefully slide them toward the closed end. Do not let any slide off.

Step 4. Before trimming the excess class tippet loop, form a lock above the Albright with a Triple Half Hitch on the class tippet.

Step 5. Tighten.

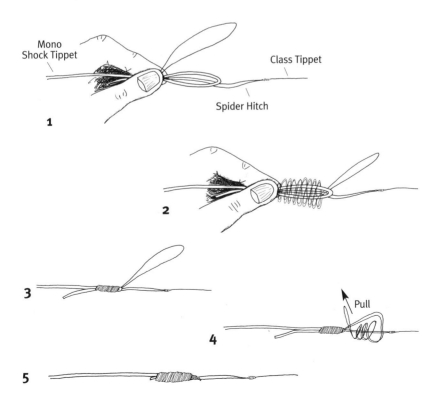

Mono Shock Tippet

Class Tippet

Spider Hitch

Pull

A Note about Mono Shock Tippet

Mono shock tippet is stiff and holds a great deal of spool memory, usually in curls. To prepare it for easier use, take 20 feet of mono shock tippet from its spool. Cut it into 18-inch sections and dip them into boiling water. When removed, they will be limp. Dry the sections in a straightened position and store them until needed in a 19-inch piece of 1/2-inch-diameter PVC tubing marked with the pound test. PVC tubing is available at most hardware stores.

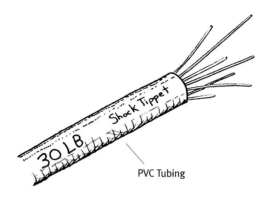

PVC Tubing

Type C Leader

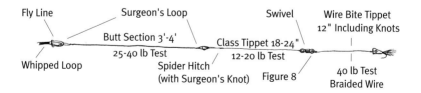

Fly Line
Surgeon's Loop
Swivel
Wire Bite Tippet
12" Including Knots
Butt Section 3'-4'
Class Tippet 18-24"
25-40 lb Test
12-20 lb Test
Whipped Loop
Spider Hitch
(with Surgeon's Knot)
Figure 8
40 lb Test
Braided Wire

The last leader, a Type C, uses a wire bite tippet in place of a mono shock tippet. As with the Type B leader, you should build this yourself. It is for aggressive fish with sharp teeth that aren't spooky or haven't learned to be wary. These include northern pike, muskellunge, tiger muskies, gar, and bowfin, as well as exotics such as the machaca, piranha, payara, and tigerfish. Because their teeth can easily shear through heavy mono, you need wire shock tippets.

There are two types of wire available—solid and braided. Solid wire is a single strand of wire available in a wide range of strengths. It is the choice of saltwater anglers because during long battles it does not wear out, but it is laborious to cast and tying knots with it is difficult. Braided wire is a group of intertwined strands of light, solid wire. Although it also hinders casting, tying knots with it is easy because it is pliable, and it can handle any of the toothy freshwater species. I find that 40-pound-test braided wire is a good all-around choice. Place a swivel between the class tippet and the wire. Flies attached to wire often twist the leader. The swivel will reduce, if not eliminate, this problem.

The only new knot you need to learn for the Type C leader is the Figure 8. It attaches the swivel and the fly to the braided wire bite tippet.

Figure-8 Knot

Step 1. Push 4 inches of the wire tag end through the eye of the fly and form a loop against the standing wire. Take the tag end around the standing wire and push it through the loop you created in the wire running through the eye.

Step 2. Using a pair of pliers, tighten the knot by pulling on the tag end. Do not pull on the standing line. It's fine to hold the standing line firmly, but tightening from this strand will form a kink in your wire shock tippet.

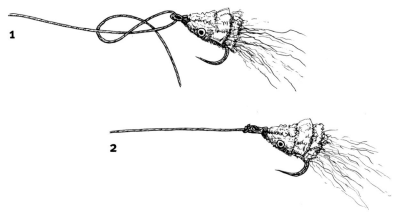

Although I always use a swivel, some anglers do not like to use them between the class tippet and the wire bite tippet because it adds weight and wind resistance to the leader. If you choose not to use a swivel, or if you don't have one, you can use the Albright Special Knot to attach the class tippet to the wire.

The northern pike's mouth full of jagged teeth can easily bite through the tippet of a Type A leader. The Yampa River, Colorado.

A Note on Type C Leaders

You will notice that the Type C leader is difficult to cast. If you keep it short, it will cast easier. Most of the time, a fish that will take a fly attached to a wire tippet isn't frightened by the fly line. You can eliminate the butt section altogether and fish with a leader of less than 3 feet. Also, use the shortest piece of wire that you can, but don't go too short. Members of the pike family like to inhale flies, and lip hooking them is rare. When I fish for northern pike, I use a piece of wire about an inch longer than the length of an average-sized pike's head. Usually, that's often less than 6 inches between class tippet and fly.

TIPS ON KNOTS

1.   Once you have completed a knot, but before you have tightened it, moisten it with water, saliva, or a commercial knot lubricant so it slides together with less friction. This reduces the loss of strength because of the heat and abrasion of friction.

2.   Use pliers to tighten all knots involving heavy mono shock tippets. You cannot tighten them sufficiently by hand.

3.   When trimming a knot, remember that mono will shrink and expand with temperature. Do not trim so closely that it will unravel.

4. Test all completed knots with a solid, constant tug. Loops should be tested by inserting a smooth object in them and pulling firmly.

5. If you are concerned with an International Game Fish Association or a National Fresh Water Fishing Hall of Fame record, Type B and C leaders have some required specifications. The class tippet must be at least 15 inches long between the connecting knots, and the shock or bite tippet may not exceed 12 inches, including the knots.

6. Tie your class tippets in advance, before going fishing. Tying the class tippet to a shock tippet is easy, but time-consuming. Imagine yourself on a weeklong adventure, the trip of a lifetime, in a remote corner of Canada's Northwest Territories. Fishing for northern pike has been slow, but because of your persistence, you're on the water when the fishing turns on. You hook up, but it's a real monster, and in your excitement you break off your fly in seconds. There's plenty more pike in casting range, but now you need to rerig, and soon it will be time to return to the lodge.

What if these knots were already done? When I purchase a spool of tippet, say 16-pound-test material, I pull it all off. I then cut it into 40-inch to 50-inch sections and tie a loop (either the Spider Hitch or Bimini Twist) on every loose end. When these are completed, I loop-to-loop all the class tippets together, stretch them across the room, and touch the knot of each loop with Zap-A-Gap cyanoacrylate glue. When the knots are dry, I wrap the daisy chain of class tippets back on the original spool.

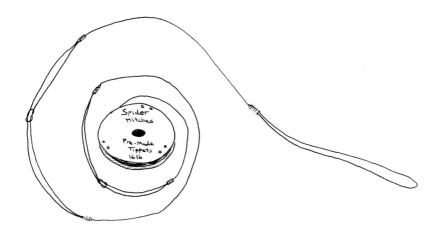

Next, I pull off sections of class tippet, add the mono or wire shock or bite tippets, and tie on the flies I expect to use. Then I take a stretcher box, a box designed to hold tippet sections with shock or bite tippets and flies already attached, and load it with as many as it will hold. To accommodate minute differences in shock tippet lengths, I use rubber bands to secure the flies. This box is almost as important as my fly rod and reel outfit. When the fishing is hot and heavy, I can change flies in seconds by pulling out a premade tippet already connected to a shock tippet with fly attached and loop it onto the butt section of my leader or the end of my fly line.

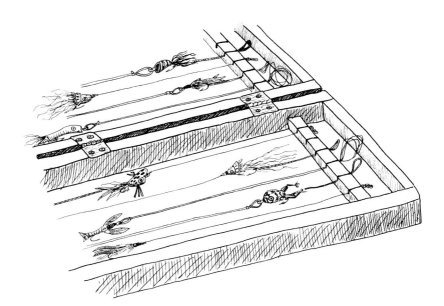

Good knots...

Lead to good fish! 18 pound grass carp. Taken by the author in downtown Phoenix.

Good casting skills are required when it comes to putting a bulky air-resistant fly where most warmwater gamefish live.

FLY CASTING

It doesn't take much experience on the water before you come to recognize the importance of good fly casting. You also learn to appreciate the importance of accurate casting, especially when fishing for certain species. For instance, sometimes the fly must land under an overhanging bush in order to reach the shade where crappies are hunting. On the other hand, tailing carp will spook when a fly lands too close. This is true with many other species, as well. In either case, a good cast with the right fly is often followed by a strike.

Like any sport, fly casting requires practice. Whether you practice on the water or in your yard, the more time you put in, the easier it becomes. A proficient fly fisher automatically knows when and where to use different types of casts, how to make them accurately, and how to cast far enough to fish efficiently. For those fly fishing for the first time, this chapter will cover the basics of fly-rod and fly-line handling, the overhead cast, how to strip in the fly, and the roll cast. But like any sport, fly casting rewards repeated attention to the basics, so even accomplished fly fishers may find something to recall here. The chapter also covers the advanced technique known as the double haul, which will help you increase your casting distance and efficiency when casting commonly used air-resistant warmwater flies.

THE START-UP POSITION

If you are right-handed, hold the fly rod by the cork handle with your right hand (rod hand) with your thumb on top. Using your forefinger (trigger finger), secure the fly line against the cork handle. With your left hand (line hand), pinch the fly line between your forefinger and thumb and hold it down and away from the reel. The rod should be pointed in the direction you plan to cast and angled slightly downward. If the rod were the hand of a clock, it would be at the eight o'clock position.

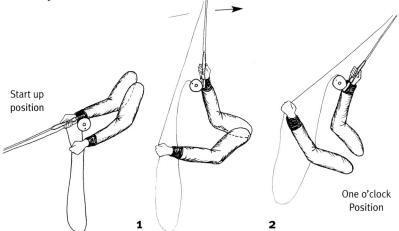

Start up position

1

2

One o'clock Position

THE OVERHEAD CAST

This is the simplest and most commonly used fly cast. It begins with a combination of backward and forward strokes. The goal is to load the fly rod, meaning that the weight of the fly line must flex the rod much like an archer flexes a bow to propel the object, the arrow or fly line, forward. Begin with about twenty feet of fly line out from the rod tip and a 7 1/2-foot leader with a piece of yarn attached to simulate a fly.

Step 1. Beginning from the start-up position, drop the fly line from the trigger finger of the rod hand so that only the line hand is holding line. Using the strength of your forearm and only a slight flick of the wrist; flip the rod and line back. This is the back cast.

Step 2. Stop at what would be considered one o'clock if the rod were the arm of a clock.

Step 3. Hesitate there long enough for the fly line to pass over the top of the rod in a shape like a U tipped ninety degrees (the loop) until it straightens out behind you, thus loading the rod.

Step 4. Using the same flick of the rod used to reach the one o'clock position, proceed forward and stop at the ten o'clock position. This is the forward cast.

Step 5. Just as you did at one o'clock, hesitate until the forward-moving loop straightens and loads the rod.

Step 6. To complete the cast, simply follow through in your forward cast, back to the start-up position at eight o'clock.

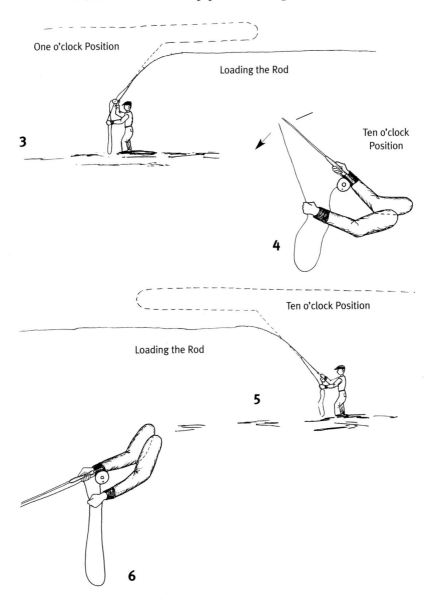

One o'clock Position

Loading the Rod

3

Ten o'clock Position

4

Ten o'clock Position

Loading the Rod

5

6

Note: **a.** If the back cast in Step 1 is performed too slowly, the loop will be too wide and won't load the rod. Hence, the cast is lost, and you must begin over.

b. If the rod extends past one o'clock, say to three o'clock, the rod is at an angle in which it cannot load. Also, the loop will be lost.

Practice the overhead cast by repeating the motion from ten o'clock to one o'clock and one o'clock to ten o'clock continuously until you actually feel the rod load. **This is called false casting**.

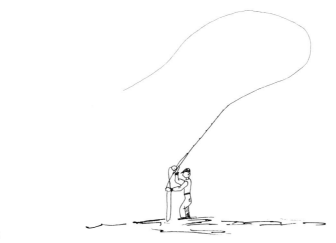

a

b

ADDING DISTANCE

When you are comfortable with the overhead cast using about twenty feet of fly line, increase your distance by letting a few feet of line slide through your line hand as it straightens and loads the rod in the ten o'clock position. Just before the rod unloads, pinch the fly line again and proceed back to one o'clock. Each time you're in the ten o'clock position, let more line out until you have enough to reach your target. On the final false cast, let the line slide through the line hand as usual at the ten o'clock position, but follow through to eight o'clock to complete the cast. You'll be amazed at how much line traveled out. **This is called shooting line.**

RETRIEVING THE FLY AND LINE

After a good overhead cast, you just might find 40 feet of fly line on the water in front of you. Without an oversized fly rod combined with the double-haul technique that you will learn later in this chapter, it is nearly impossible to begin another overhead cast because of the weight of the line and the resistance caused by the water's surface tension on this much line. Therefore, you must bring the fly line back in 20 feet. Retrieving the line to recast is the same as retrieving the fly to fool the fish. **The method used is called stripping.**

From the start-up position, let go of the fly line in the line hand and reach for it just below your trigger finger from the rod hand. Pull the line downward with the line hand, letting the line slide under your trigger finger, thus bringing in the fly line and fly. When stripping to recast, pull large lengths of line with the line hand to get it in fast to prepare for the next cast, but when retrieving the fly to entice a strike from a fish, shorter strips may be required. For instance, when retrieving a popper for a large-mouth bass, I do a quick 10-inch strip (the quickness makes the fly pop) and hesitate for a few seconds. If stripping in a damselfly nymph to fool a jumbo yellow perch, I do steady, inch-long strips.

THE ROLL CAST

Occasionally, the basic overhead cast is impossible because of obstructions behind you. The roll cast solves this problem. Unlike the overhead cast, the roll cast should be practiced on the water, because the surface tension gives the resistance needed to load the rod. Begin with about fifteen feet of fly line out from the rod tip and a 7 1/2-foot leader with a piece of yarn to simulate a fly.

Step 1. Beginning from the start-up position, drop the fly line from the trigger finger so that only the line hand is holding the line. Raise your rod, but this time do it slowly, and just until it is slightly past the twelve o'clock position, then hesitate. The belly of the line should be dangling slightly behind your elbow while the majority should be in the water, held by the water tension.

Step 2. Drive the rod forward and downward with your forearm and a slight flick of the wrist to the ten o'clock position. As the fly line rolls forward, follow through, ending at the eight o'clock or start-up position.

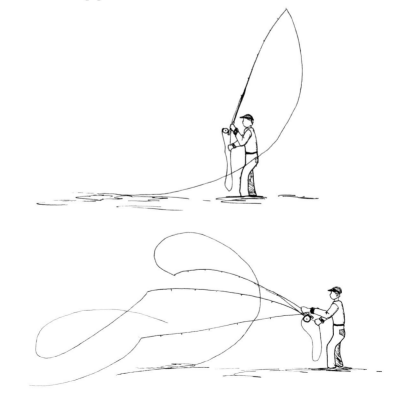

1

2

Unlike the overhead cast, the roll cast doesn't have any form of false casting. It is basically a one-shot deal. Therefore, the distance achieved is less than that of the overhead cast. Nonetheless, it gets the fly to the fish when a thick canopy of trees or other vegetation obstructs a back cast.

The roll cast can also be used to prepare for an overhead cast with a sinking fly line. These dense lines, which are usually attached to a heavy fly, as well, are difficult to lift from the water, and often the first motion of an overhead cast isn't enough to do so. The roll cast brings the sunken fly and fly line to the surface so that there is less water resistance for the start of the overhead cast. Simply make a roll cast and, without stopping, go immediately into an overhead cast.

Once you can perform the overhead cast and the roll cast well, you should expand your skills. An advanced fly-casting technique called the double haul will increase your line speed. More line speed means more load on the rod, which in turn means that fewer false casts are needed to reach longer casting distances. It even makes it easier to cast in the wind and to cast large, air-resistant flies. It also helps with casting accuracy.

THE DOUBLE HAUL

I recommend that you practice the motions of the double haul with just your hands and a pencil until you feel comfortable. Get the rhythm down in slow motion first, then increase your speed gradually until you attain a normal false-casting pace. Finally, add the rod, reel, and line and try the technique in your back yard. Most anglers who master the double haul use it routinely, even with lighter rods on small rivers.

Step 1. Begin the cast with the rod tip close to the water. Strip in any slack in the fly line. This will allow for a powerful pickup and back cast that will load the rod efficiently from the beginning.

Step 2. As you start the back cast, simultaneously jerk the line hand downward just a few inches. This rapid line hand movement increases both the line speed and the loading of the rod. This is the first of two such movements called hauls. You also can use this single haul to accelerate the line and help load the rod on a simple overhead cast.

Step 3. Quickly return the line hand close to the rod hand, where it remains during the pause between the back cast and the forward cast at the one o'clock position. Hold the fly line tightly and prepare for the second haul.

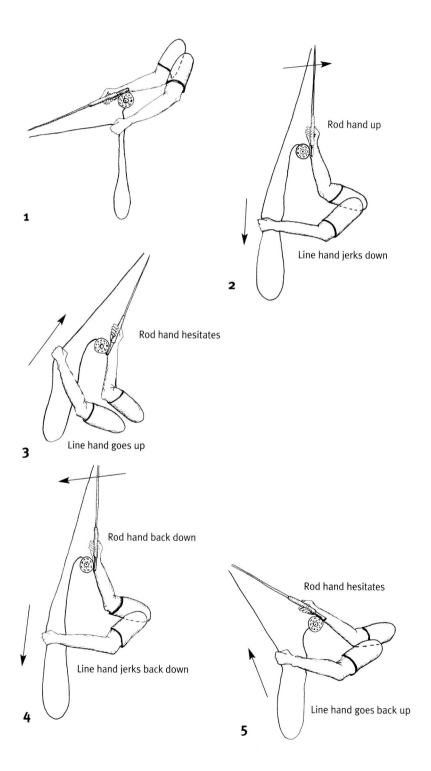

1

Rod hand up

Line hand jerks down

2

Rod hand hesitates

Line hand goes up

3

Rod hand back down

Line hand jerks back down

4

Rod hand hesitates

Line hand goes back up

5

Step 4. At the start of the forward cast, simultaneously jerk the line hand downward again. This second haul again increases line speed and the load on the rod.

Step 5. Again, the line hand returns close to the rod hand during the pause between forward cast and back cast at the ten o'clock position. This time, while controlling the line with the line hand's thumb and forefinger, allow line to slide out, lengthening the false cast. Then, when the maximum desired release of line is attained, close the line hand tightly on the line and repeat the process until the preferred casting distance is reached. On the final false cast, shoot line while returning to eight o'clock, as you would when shooting line on the final stroke in the overhead cast. Because of the extra line speed created by the double haul, nearly twice the amount of line should travel out.

DOUBLE HAUL TIPS

1. Hold the line tightly. The increased line speed and loading from the haul often cause the line to slip through your fingers too soon, especially when the line is wet.

2. A powerful haul-aided forward cast often kicks the accelerating line around the rod butt or the reel. To avoid this, upon delivering the fly on your final cast, guide the accelerating fly line while it slips through your line hand. This will prevent tangling and allow you to start stripping in the fly as soon as the fly settles on the surface.

3. Leader length, fly size, and wind direction, among other things, will affect your casting. Add the excitement of seeing a fine fish and you'll realize that it takes practice and experience to manage all the elements of a double haul. Remember that larger rods, lines, and flies take a little more time and effort to develop the casting dynamics that you may be familiar with from using lighter tackle. Be patient with yourself.

SHOOTING LINE ON THE BACK CAST

Although the double haul is the most powerful method of casting, another way to make a quick cast is by letting a few feet of line slip out of your hand during the back cast. You can do this when making either a single haul or a double haul cast. The additional bit of airborne line increases the loading of the rod while also reducing the amount of line you need to shoot on the forward cast. Start by letting only a foot or two of line loose. Slipping too much line on the back cast will hurt your timing and may bog down the forward cast.

The vegetation of a pond can make landing a fish difficult.

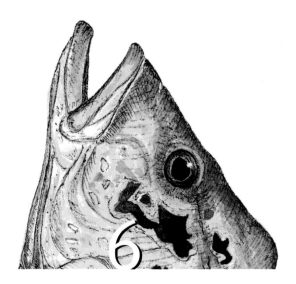

HOOKING AND LANDING FISH

Once the cast is made and the fly has landed in the water, you are fishing. Now you must learn how to hook the fish and improve your odds of landing it. As you might expect, given the variety of warmwater fish, from bluegills to muskellunge, the different types of water they inhabit, and the different techniques you can employ in fishing for them, how you hook and land a fish depends on a lot of different factors, including how a particular species tends to take the fly, where the fly is being fished in the water column, and the ways different species respond to being hooked.

With many members of the sunfish family, you may get an immediate strike. Therefore, you must be in position to set the hook. To be in this position when the fly hits the water, with the line hand, simply hook the fly line under your trigger finger as you are following through in your forward cast from the ten o'clock position to the eight o'clock position. If you put yourself in the start-up position for casting, you're also ready to set the hook.

If you're fishing a dry fly or a popper, set the hook by raising the rod tip over your shoulder as if to make a back cast, while pulling down with the line hand in one large strip. If you miss the strike, consider it the beginning of an overhead cast and drop the fly back to the fish by just continuing the casting motion. The fly should return to where the strike occurred, and if you're lucky, either the same fish will eat it again, perhaps thinking that its prey escaped only momentarily, or another fish traveling with the first will take it.

With subsurface flies, I set the hook differently. The over-the-shoulder hook set that I use for the popper pulls the fly away from the feeding fish if it doesn't connect, and if this occurs in deep water, there is no way to get the fly back to the fish in an instant, as you can with a surface fly. Instead, you need to set the hook by stripping until you feel the fly hooking the fish, and then drive the hook deeper by jerking the rod to the side. Should the fly pull free, it is still within sight of the fish, as well as available to others that might be following. You'll have a second chance. For a soft-mouthed species such as the white crappie, this combination of a strip and rod jerk should hook the fish to land it. For a hard-mouthed fish such as the muskie, aggressively repeat the rod jerk one more time.

Once you have hooked the fish, you must play it properly in order to tire it for landing. With most freshwater fish, a blistering run is unlikely, and loose fly line accumulated while stripping may lie around you. With a panfish, I simply leave it there, and with my rod tip high, fight the fish by stripping line in with my line hand, if necessary letting it slide back out through the trigger finger of my rod hand. My hands basically take the place of the reel.

With a larger fish such as a hefty northern pike or a girthy 25-pound grass carp, loose line must be handled differently. The initial run can be fast and furious. Hold the rod tip high and allow the fish to go. Loose line that was stripped in before the strike will leave the boat deck or water at the same speed as the fish runs. Be sure the line has a clear path by guiding it away from the reel and rod butt with your hand. And try to keep it clear of obstructions—including parts of your own body—in the first place. Fly lines obey Murphy's Law and wrap around anything they possibly can, usually at the worst possible moment. This is especially true in boats. Try to eliminate line-tangling protuberances in advance. It's easier than undoing a tangle with a big fish pulling on the line.

The reel's drag, as well as the trailing fly line and backing, will begin to tire the fish. When the fish slows or stops, add pressure by increasing the bend in the rod. Gain back all the line possible using a smooth pumping motion. Lift the rod firmly, then move the tip back toward the fish and reel in slack repeatedly. Pinch the line with your rod hand while reeling with the other hand. Try to guide the backing and fly line evenly onto the reel.

Releasing a brute striped bass.

The key to landing a fish as fast as possible so as to be able to release it in good shape is to continue to apply pressure to the fish while often changing the angle of the rod. This forces the fish to keep changing its angle to you, never allowing it a moment's rest. Be prepared to let the fish run again whenever you feel a sudden surge, though. A 10-pound tiger muskie may take 15 minutes to land for a beginner, while the more experienced angler lands it in 5. A fish landed in 5 minutes as opposed to 15 has a much better chance of surviving after release. Keep the pressure on.

There are many members of the sunfish family and in this New England pond more than one can be caught at a time. Top: Pumpkinseed sunfish. Bottom: A very dark colored bluegill.

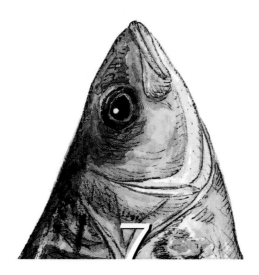

POPULAR WARMWATER SPECIES

What follows is a list of fifteen commonly sought-after warmwater species with color illustrations so you can identify them immediately. Listed with each species are some important facts, their range, the water type in which they reside, size, habitat preferences, food preferences, handling concerns, recommended tackle, and effective fly patterns used to catch them. Also included is valuable information about tactics to catch these species.

THE SUNFISH FAMILY (CENTRARCHIDAE)

The sunfish family makes up a large majority of the most commonly sought-after warmwater fishes. The smaller members, often known as panfish, consist of the ever-popular bluegill, a native to most of North America, and its closely related cousins found regionally, the pumpkinseed, longear, redear (shellcracker), redbreast, green, orangespotted, flier, mud, and dollar sunfish. There are also a few that are rarely fished for because of their minute size, 3 inches in length or less: the pygmy, banded, bluespotted, and bantam sunfish. Add in a few hybrids from lakes and ponds where several species exist together, and wow!

What many anglers don't realize is that this family also includes the largemouth, smallmouth, Suwannee, Guadalupe, spotted, and redeye bass, as well as the rock bass, warmouth (goggle-eye), Sacramento perch, and both the black and white crappie. The bluegill, black crappie, largemouth bass and smallmouth bass are the best-known members of the sunfish family and the ones most often pursued. Information I give to help catch these species should apply to their close cousins, as well.

The Bluegill (Bream or Sun Perch)

Notes: The most common and perhaps the most sought-after of the smaller sunfish, bluegills are abundant wherever found and usually they are easy to catch. However, bluegills over a pound can tantalize any flyrodder. Pound for pound, the bluegill is one of the hardest-fighting fish.

Range: Native east of the Rocky Mountains to the Atlantic coast from southern Canada to Texas and Florida. Introduced in the Rocky Mountain and West Coast states and even in ponds and lakes of Hawaii.

Water Types: Ponds, lakes, rivers, and canals.

Size: Commonly reaches 6 inches in length and less than a pound, but 10-inchers weighing a pound or more are taken regularly. Mammoth bluegills have topped scales at over 2 pounds, with the world record at 4 1/2 pounds!

Habitat Preference: Water from 3 to 12 feet deep anywhere structure is found, such as drop-offs, sunken logs, rocks, lily pads and other aquatic plants, as well as under overhanging bushes or trees, docks, swimming rafts, and boats.

Food Preferences: Some vegetation, insects, snails, freshwater shrimp, freshwater mussels, small crayfish, leeches, minnows, the eggs

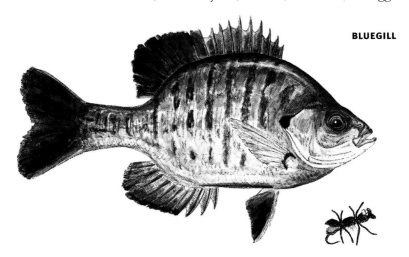

BLUEGILL

and fry of other fish, and so on. Generally, these opportunistic feeders will hit any moving target up to their own size.

Handling Concerns: Avoid the spines in the dorsal and anal fins.

Close Cousins: The pumpkinseed, longear, redear, redbreast, green, orangespotted, flier, mud, and dollar sunfish, along with the warmouth and rock bass.

Recommended Tackle: (based on an 8-inch, 3/4-pound bluegill).

> **Rod:** 9-foot for a 4-weight line.
>
> **Reel:** Bluegills are known for using their dinner-plate body shape to fight hard on light tackle, but long runs do not occur. A basic reel with a single-pawl or dual-pawl drag system is sufficient.
>
> **Line:** 4-weight, weight-forward, floating—WF4F.
>
> **Leader:** Type A, 7 1/2-foot, 4-pound to 6-pound tippet.
>
> **Flies:** The best hook sizes are from 10 to 18. As a general rule, I fish brightly colored flies during a sunny day because they stand out. During periods of low light, I fish dark colors because they show a more distinct silhouette than light colors under those conditions. Excellent patterns include the Standard Popper, Chernobyl Ant, Dave's Hopper, Woolly Bugger, Beadhead Rubber-Leg Hare's Ear Nymph, and the Sanchez Damsel Nymph. Weed guards will help in many situations.

Tactics

It is hard for me to pass up the fantastic top-water opportunities for bluegills. I always begin my pursuit with a brightly colored popper, about a size 14, and prospect blindly over weed beds, lily pads, stumps, or any other reachable structure. Only on rare occasions will this not lead to instant results.

When bluegills are skeptical of a top-water fly, observe their behavior closely. Frequently they will stare curiously at the fly from several inches away, often in a small gang of three to six. If this occurs, remain patient and do not move the popper. One of the fish may still attack. If they hold back and seem to lose interest, give the fly a tiny twitch. This will regain their attention, and only seldom does it not induce an automatic strike.

I have fished ponds with large, selective bluegills that will not eat top-water flies. Usually they are selective because of fishing pressure. Frequent changes of flies, both surface and subsurface types, and frequent changes of retrieve methods may finally prevail.

Many private bass ponds have big bluegills that are more like pets than wild fish because they are fed fish pellets on a regular basis. In these situations, be ready for a serious standoff. If you had the choice of having to work every day without even being sure of getting a decent meal or of taking all day, every day off and having luxurious feasts delivered to you regularly, what would you pick? Getting an overgrown, spoiled-rotten bluegill to move for a popper is out of the question. However, a popper is entertaining to look at, and what if a pellet fly dangled a foot below? A trick that I use is to tie a Beadhead Rubber-Leg Hare's Ear Nymph about eighteen inches behind my popper. My theory is that the popper attracts the fish by making a splashing sound like pellets being released, and then the nymph looks to them like a sinking pellet.

Dangling a nymph below a popper not only works on bluegill, but on most sunfish family members including this redbreast sunfish.

Bluegills also eat minnows and the fry of other gamefish. A small streamer or a small Clouser Deep Minnow can be deadly. Damselfly nymphs seem to be regarded as a delicacy. Land an olive damsel pattern against a log or along a bed of lily pads and let it sink. Add in an occasional inch-long strip, and wham!

Once you locate one bluegill, you have located many. These pint-sized fish live in packs. If you're not satisfied with the average size, don't move on too soon. Chances are that some big ones lurk in the area, but can't beat the aggressive smaller ones to the fly. Eventually, after you catch a number of the small ones, the big ones might appear. To find larger fish, cast to slightly deeper areas bordering where the little guys hang out, and be ready.

The Black Crappie (Calico Bass, Papermouth, Sac-á-Lait, or Speckled Perch)

Notes: A popular panfish for the dinner plate. Perhaps that's why they are often wilier than their easily caught cousins.

Range: Native to the upper Mississippi Valley and Great Lakes region and southward to Florida and Texas. Introduced in the Rocky Mountain and West Coast states, as well as in New England and parts of Canada.

Water Types: Ponds, lakes, rivers, and canals.

Size: There are 10-inchers lurking in most schools of crappies, but 13-inchers of a pound or better are not uncommon. Record catches have exceeded 4 pounds.

Habitat Preference: Water from 6 feet or less to 30 feet. They prefer weeds and other structures, such as sunken brush piles, fallen timber, and riprap. They also hide near drop-offs and humps, as well as under docks, moored boats, rafts, and bridges.

Food Preferences: Minnows are their favorite meal, but insects, freshwater shrimp, leeches, and plankton are also included.

Handling Concerns: Avoid the spines in the dorsal and anal fins.

Close Cousin: The white crappie.

Recommended Tackle: (based on a 13-inch, 1-pound crappie).

> **Rod**: 9-foot for a 5-weight line.
>
> **Reel:** Although crappies tug hard, long runs do not occur. A basic reel with a single-pawl or dual-pawl drag system is sufficient.

BLACK CRAPPIE

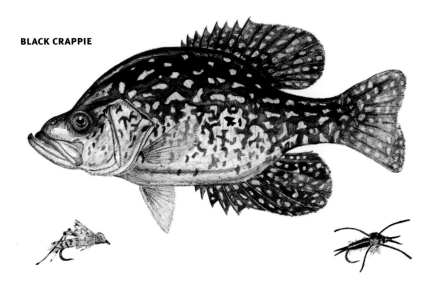

Line: 5-weight, weight-forward, floating—WF5F.
Leader: Type A, 7 1/2-foot, 4-pound to 8-pound tippet.
Flies: The best hook sizes are from 6 to 12. I do most my crappie fishing after sunset and find flies tied in black to be excellent because they show up better to the fish under low-light conditions, but in bright conditions, try white, yellow, or chartreuse. Excellent patterns include the Conehead Mohair Leech, Clouser Deep Minnow, Woolly Bugger, and Beadhead Rubber-Leg Hare's Ear Nymph, but don't hesitate to use surface flies such as Standard Poppers, Chernobyl Ants, and Dave's Hoppers.

Tactics

Locating crappies can be more difficult than locating other members of the sunfish family. The easiest time to target crappies is in the spring, just after ice-out, or when water temperatures approach the 60-degree mark. This is in and around spawning time, and they will predictably be in the shallows over gravel, near weeds, or in the thickest of underwater brush piles. Because minnows are the main ingredient in a crappie's diet, begin with a fly you can strip in, such as a Clouser Deep Minnow or black Woolly Bugger, about a size 10. Once you've located crappies, continue to fish that area. They nearly always congregate in schools, and when they are on the feed, they can be caught one after another.

After spawning ends, crappies move to deeper, cooler water for the warm summer months. Often they will find enough minnows and other food sources to survive at depths of over 30 feet and are difficult to find. Dredging conehead-style flies on sinking lines will work, but can be a tedious method of catching crappies, even if you're are lucky enough to locate them in the first place.

At that time of year, I concentrate my efforts on just a couple hours of fishing at the end of the day. Water temperature typically cools enough after sunset for crappies to move into the shallows and hunt. Although not as effective as any of the minnow patterns, my favorite fly for such conditions is a small Standard Popper. Cast it over weed beds and sunken trees in 10 to 15 feet of water. Swimming rafts and moored boats also are particularly good places to find hunting crappies. Cast to these areas, pop the fly, and patiently let it sit for at least 5 seconds, often even longer. Then pop it again, and continue until you've slowly popped your fly 10 feet beyond where you believe the crappies to be.

Crappies do not usually eat the popper on the first attempt, so make repeated casts to likely locations.

In New England, where I grew up, and in Wisconsin and Minnesota, where I went to college, I did a lot of fishing at night under boat-dock lights and street lights along bridges. Night lights attract numerous insects, particularly moths, and during the right time of year, they attract various mayflies, as well as minnows that come to eat them. These are particularly good times to fly fish for crappies because, as I mentioned earlier, insects and minnows are a major part of their diet.

The Largemouth Bass (Black Bass, Bucketmouth, or Green Trout)

Notes: Perhaps the most popular freshwater gamefish in North America by virtue of its wide distribution and willingness to take almost any type of bait, lure, or fly.

Range: Native east of the Rocky Mountains from southern Canada to northern Mexico and all the way to the East Coast from New York to Florida. With the exception of Alaska they have been introduced in every U.S. state, including Hawaii, as well as in parts of Central America, Europe, Africa, and Japan.

Water Types: Ponds, lakes, rivers, and canals.

Size: Commonly reaches 20 inches and over 5 pounds, but where year-round feeding and growth occurs, most often in its southern range, largemouths get much bigger. Largemouths surpassing 10 pounds are caught, and fish over 20 pounds have been recorded.

Habitat Preference: Water from 4 to 15 feet deep among beds of lily pads and other weeds, with scattered structure. Submerged trees, brush piles, tires, cars, and old docks provide protection. Reservoirs with standing trees, fence lines, buildings, and other underwater artificial structure are like castles to a largemouth colony.

Food Preferences: Largemouth bass are far from finicky. Minnows, smaller members of the sunfish family, perch, crayfish, leeches, insects, salamanders, lizards, baby turtles, frogs, mice, snakes, ducklings, and even small birds that fall from nests at the water's edge are fair game.

Handling Concerns: Avoid the spines in the dorsal and anal fins.

Close Cousins: The Suwannee, Guadalupe, spotted, smallmouth, and redeye bass.

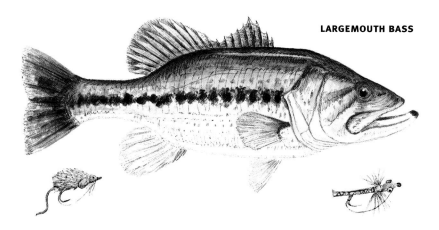

LARGEMOUTH BASS

Recommended Tackle: (based on a 5-pound largemouth).

> **Rod**: 9-foot for a 7-weight line.
>
> **Reel**: Largemouths are not known for long screaming runs, so backing is of minimal importance, but these fish are brawny fighters. A reel with a strong, smooth drag will help when trophy largemouths attempt to retreat home.
>
> **Line**: 7-weight, weight-forward, floating—WF7F.
>
> **Leader**: Type A, 7 1/2foot, 10-pound to 16-pound tippet.
>
> **Flies**: The best hook sizes are from 2 to 8. I prefer to use bright colors during a sunny day and resort to black, dark brown, and olive in periods of lower light. Excellent patterns include the Standard Popper, Prism Diver, Swimming Frog, Mouserat, Spent Damsel Dragon, Dave's Hopper, Chernobyl Ant, Clouser Deep Minnow, Sanchez's Conehead the Barbarian, and the Sanchez Double Bunny. Be sure these are tied with weed guards.

Tactics

Except during the cold of the early spring or late fall, which slows down the metabolism of the bass and limits their predatory instinct to simple, slow-moving targets, I begin my approach to largemouth bass with top-water flies. Hardly ever can a largemouth hold back from lashing out for a delicious frog traveling to neighboring lily pads or an exhausted mouse swimming for a distant shoreline. Busting along the surface with any of the popper-style flies mentioned above will attract the attention of a largemouth bass.

Stripping a surface fly should always be done in a way that best imitates the animal your fly resembles. Imagine real frogs swimming.

They move from floating on the surface to diving under, then, in one elongated body stroke, they push and glide back to the surface, where they usually sit motionless for a few seconds. Any Standard Popper, Prism Diver, or a Swimming Frog can be made to imitate that exact motion. Simply make a smooth strip of 2 to 3 feet and let the fly float back to the surface. Don't strip again too quickly. Largemouths love to smash a fly that has come to rest after a strip because the pause exactly imitates what a frog does. Some old-timers insist that before the next strip, you should wait until the ripples from your last pop go completely away. Repeat this presentation through a largemouth's territory several times and your popper will get crushed!

Mouse patterns, Chernobyl Ants, and Dave's Hoppers are fished on the surface as well, but the action imparted to them should be different. Only amphibians and reptiles move gracefully through the water. A mouse, dying insect, or drowning bird struggles. Make your fly struggle. I like to do a quick, 6-inch strip with a mouse or a terrestrial pattern, creating a bubbly, splashy noise, then let it sit for only a second and

This greedy little largemouth took a fly despite the fact that he already had a mouthful of tiny shad that he preyed upon seconds before.

wiggle it with some mere inch-long strips. Then I let it sit for a few seconds and do another quick pop. Land these flies close to protruding logs, brush piles, boulders, between beds of lily pads, under trees, and any other likely place that a land-based creature is apt to enter the water. With weedless flies, you can land the fly on top of a log or over a tree branch. Let it dangle a few seconds, teasing any watching fish, and then drag it off. This is such a realistic presentation that you better hold onto your shorts when the fly touches down on the water!

Fishing subsurface flies for largemouth bass is also effective, but can be difficult, thanks to the weedy, brushy cover in which they thrive. Even with supposedly weedless flies, it seems that hook points find ways to hang up on logs and sunken brush and manage to cling to pieces of weed, grass, and twigs. Nonetheless, largemouths frequently feed on other fishes, leeches, and aquatic insects. Therefore, wet flies will catch them.

I resort to subsurface flies when the cold slows down the bass in the spring and again in the fall. Double Bunnies, Clouser Deep Minnows, and a variety of leech patterns stripped slowly produce the most strikes. Fortunately, most weed beds and lily beds don't grow thick during cold seasons, and less snagging occurs, but the relative lack of weeds can also make finding largemouth bass difficult.

I target the areas where I find bass in the summer months. Often, regardless of the lack of weeds, largemouths remain in these locations because of other sunken debris—perhaps a hollowed tree trunk or a truck tire or irrigation pipe that were hidden by the plentiful vegetation. If you can't find the bass there, you will need to explore new locations. Prospecting in deeper water than usual, as deep as 15 feet, may be necessary.

The Smallmouth Bass (Smallie or Bronzeback)

Notes: Another favorite North American freshwater gamefish, the smallmouth bass is best known for its fighting ability and acrobatic jumps.

Range: Native east of the Rocky Mountains from southern Canada as far south as Kansas, eastward to North Carolina and north to Maine and southern Quebec. Smallmouths have since been introduced in many other states, including Oregon and Washington in the Columbia River drainage, where the species thrives.

Water Types: Lakes and rivers.

Size: Commonly reaches 16 inches and 2 pounds, with 20-inch fish weighing 4 to 5 pounds occasionally taken. At age five, I watched my dad land a 25-inch, 8-pound trophy. He was so excited that he jumped up and down in the family rowboat, only to cause a major leak that nearly ended in us sinking. I am certain that if the choice had arisen, he would have saved his catch and let me fend for myself.

Habitat Preference: Water from 5 to 20 feet deep, except during spawning, when the smallmouth moves to water as little as 2 feet deep

SMALLMOUTH BASS

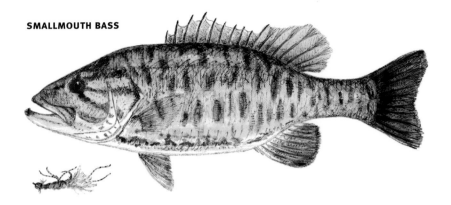

to build and guard its nest. Unlike its cousins, the smallmouth prefers the cool, clear water of lakes and of the riffles in rivers. Structure is the key to locating smallmouths. Rather than weeds, smallmouths prefer areas with sunken timber, boulders, and gravel bottoms.

Food Preferences: Like the largemouth, the smallmouth will eat almost any moving creature of the correct size, but hands down, crayfish are its favorite meal.

Handling Concerns: Avoid the spines in the dorsal and anal fins.

Close Cousins: The redeye, spotted, largemouth, Suwannee, and Guadalupe bass.

Recommended Tackle: (based on a 16-inch, 2-pound smallmouth).

    Rod: 9-foot for a 6-weight line.

    Reel: It is unlikely that a smallmouth would pull heaps of line off the reel and thus require backing to keep him hooked. Nonetheless, these guys pull hard and usually hit the air a few times before dashing straight for boulders or a hollow log. A reel with a strong, smooth drag will help against a short but feisty run.

    Line: 6-weight, weight-forward, floating—WF6F.

    Leader: Type A, 9-foot, 10-pound to 16-pound tippet.

    Flies: The best hook sizes are from 4 to 8. With surface flies, I have fished every imaginable color and it seems to matter little, but with subsurface flies, orange, olive, brown, rust, and black work well, alone or in any combination. Excellent patterns include the Standard Popper, Sanchez Crawdaddy, Whitlock's Softshell Crayfish, Conehead Mohair Leech, Clouser Deep Minnow, and the Beadhead Rubber-Leg Kaufmann Stone.

Tactics

I grew up fly fishing for smallmouth bass. Every summer of my life until I was 20 years old was spent at the family summer cottage on Lake Winnipesaukee in Wolfeboro, New Hampshire. Starting the day I was old enough, I could be found popping the shallows either from boat-yard piers or our 16-foot canoe on a glassy-smooth lake before sunrise and again after sunset. Practicing catch-and-release at an early age, I had pet smallies, knew what fly they would eat, and most importantly, where to find them under all weather conditions throughout the year.

Back then, my smallmouth fly-fishing season began about one month after ice-out. This is the typical starting date in all regions where smallmouths are present. Water temperatures in the shallows will have reached the low 60s, and the smallmouths will have moved there from winter depths to build nests and spawn. Incredibly protective of their eggs or fry, they will hit anything that threatens their nests, from lures and flies to the toes of unwelcome swimmers. When I was a youngster, these easy-to-catch fish were too much to resist. Every fly concoction in my box worked, and as I kept catching fish with ease, I developed my fly-fishing skills.

Eventually I outgrew this enthusiasm for spawning smallmouths when I learned that every time I removed a smallmouth from its nest, pumpkinseed sunfish and yellow perch from under our dock pilings were gobbling up the precious eggs and fry. Today, I preach against antagonizing spawning bass and encourage anglers simply to wait the two weeks it often takes until they are done protecting their nests and return to their normal feeding habits.

Normal feeding habits for smallmouths consist of searching close to their lairs, usually in 5 to 20 feet of water, for crayfish, minnows, hell-grammites, and dragonfly larvae. Consistent weather, good or bad, does not change these habits much, but changes in the weather, including cold fronts, heat waves, intense thunderstorms, and unstable condi-tions, send smallies to deep water and into a state of lockjaw. Then, even fast-sinking lines with Clouser Deep Minnows and various crayfish patterns dragged in front of their noses rarely produce results. Therefore, let's assume the tactics we are about to discuss are for normal, stable conditions.

Be prepared to fish from top to bottom. Smallies are perhaps the most aggressive top-water feeders of all, and if exciting strikes are what you live for, begin with a noisy popper. First, work the shallows in 4 to

8 feet of water. With a pair of polarized sunglasses, look for submerged boulders, logs, and other debris. Explore around rocky points, moored boats, and close to docks. A good sidearm cast that sneaks a couple feet under a covered boathouse often will draw a strike. Just don't let the owner see you do it, because not only might you snag an expensive boat cover, but you might catch the owner's pet smallie.

Cast near these objects and be ready. Although smallies sometimes will strike a fly the second it hits the water, sometimes they like to observe it for many casts. As you would when targeting largemouth bass, vary the idle time between pops. Letting the popper sit dead still for 10 seconds may not be enough. Try 15. If an area looks particularly good, work it with heart, making up to 10 casts to the same spot with altered gurgling pops on each cast. If you catch one, don't leave. Smallmouths rarely hunt alone, and often, more attempts to the same spot will produce at least another fish of comparable size.

Early mornings, evenings, and overcast days provide ideal conditions for top-water action, because fish do not feel too exposed to threats from above when the light is low. We often find ourselves fishing outside of this prime window of opportunity, however. In the middle of a bright sunny day, look for smallmouths in deeper water. Shade-producing drop-offs, shelves, humps, huge boulders, and hollow logs in an area that produces smallies early in the day also will provide action when the sun is high and beating down through the water. Also try channels or other deep water near the shallows. Just break out the sinking line and fish the depths with a conehead or crayfish pattern, or try large nymph patterns that imitate hellgrammites, damselflies, dragonflies, or even stoneflies. As you would when fishing poppers, make repeated casts with varied stripping techniques before moving to a new location.

In the southern reaches of the smallmouth's range, hot August temperatures can push them down as much as 30 feet deep, just the way a cold front will in the northern part of their range. Fortunately, this is also a great time of year to hunt them in rivers. There, the higher oxygen content and colder water temperatures keep smallies hungry and active during severe heat waves. Like trout, river smallies take advantage of aquatic hatches, and targeting these can be a great deal of fun. Blind fishing with poppers, frog imitations, and other surface flies, as well as dredging the bottom with a simple Woolly Bugger can produce amazing action.

Many anglers find it difficult to determine the difference between smallmouth and largemouth bass. Here are three key methods. First, the largemouth indeed has a bigger mouth. The upper jaw extends behind the eye, while on the smallmouth, it does not. Second, the spiny section of the largemouth's dorsal fin is nearly separated from the rear, soft section, while the smallmouth's is a continuous fin. Third, the two fish differ in color. The largemouth is black on top, which then fades to a greenish shade with a distinct horizontal band from head to tail. The smallmouth's back is bronze to copper—hence the nickname bronzeback— and it has no horizontal band on its sides.

THE TEMPERATE BASS FAMILY (PERCICHTHYIDAE)

Close relatives of the sunfish family, the temperate bass are excellent fly-rod gamefish. They willingly take both surface and subsurface flies and are liked by anglers for their fighting ability. They generally school in lakes and rivers, and once located, they can provide hours of flyrodding enjoyment. The group consists of four species: the white bass, striped bass, yellow bass, and white perch, which is in fact not related to the perch family. There is also the popular "wiper", a sterile hybrid of the white and striped bass. The white bass and the striped bass are the best-known members of the temperate bass family and the ones most often pursued. Information I give to help catch these species should apply to their close cousins, as well.

The White Bass

Notes: Over the past twenty years, the white bass has gained respect from anglers. Their fierce feeding habits, make for some of the most exciting freshwater action imaginable. They resemble many saltwater fish in the way they hunt in a school, herding and terrorizing baitfish.

Range: Native from Minnesota east to the Saint Lawrence River drainage and south to northern Alabama and Texas. They have been introduced in the Rocky Mountain states and westward to California.

Water Types: Lakes and rivers.

Size: Commonly reaches 12 inches and weighs up to a pound. Large fish of 3 pounds have been caught, and on rare occasions, record catches have topped 5 pounds.

Habitat Preference: White bass need large lakes or rivers with extensive areas over 10 feet deep. They can be found feeding in as little as 6 feet of water in a river or shallow portion of a lake, but also suspend in water as much as 40 feet down during the summer months. In rivers, they don't mind fast current and seem particularly fond of turbulent flows below a dam.

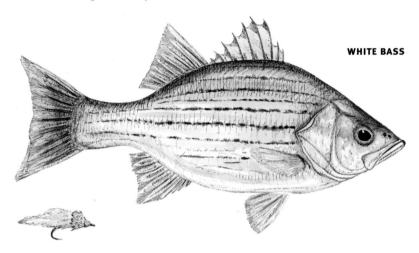

WHITE BASS

Food Preferences: White bass are voracious feeders. Minnows and other small fish, particularly shad, in the path of a large school will get eaten. Like most fish, they will take advantage of other easy meals such as insects, leeches, and other small mouthfuls.

Handling Concerns: Avoid the spines in the dorsal and anal fins. Also be careful of the razor-sharp bone on the gill plates.

Close Cousins: The white perch, yellow bass, striped bass, and "wiper", a hybrid of the striped bass and the white bass.

Recommended Tackle: (based on a 13-inch, 1-pound white bass).
    Rod: 9-foot for a 6-weight line.
    Reel: It's pretty unlikely that you would ever need backing to hold a 1-pound fish, but with a long cast, followed by an immediate hookup in fast current, you just never know. A reel with a smooth drag won't hurt.
    Line: 6-weight, weight-forward, floating—WF6F—or 6-weight, weight-forward, sinking—WF6S.
    Leader: Type A, 9-foot, 8-pound to 12-pound tippet.
    Flies: The best hook sizes are from 6 to 10. Although white is the most dependable fly color, be prepared to change to

yellow, chartreuse, olive, or black. Excellent flies include the Kiwi Muddler, Woolly Bugger, Conehead Mohair Leech, Clouser Deep Minnow, Sanchez Double Bunny, and on occasion, the Standard Popper.

Tactics

Whether you're fishing a lake or a river, if feeding white bass are in casting range, you have a good chance at catching them. White bass forage in large schools, often herding smaller baitfish such as gizzard shad and threadfin shad into tight masses. Competition among schooling fish always reduces their selectivity, and with white bass, any moving object close in size to their prey can result in hookups.

Locating schools of white bass may not be easy, though. They are roamers in the large bodies of water that they prefer. In a deep lake, especially during cold fronts and heat waves, they could be hiding anywhere, usually suspended somewhere in the middle. At these times, it is best to concentrate your efforts early or late in the day, when the white bass are likely to move to shallower water and feed. Always watch for diving gulls and terns, indicating that feeding frenzies are also taking place below a lake's surface. Because white bass often chase baitfish voraciously, it is not uncommon that their terrified prey will leap from the surface to avoid being eaten from below. That's another sign to anticipate.

In large rivers, white bass seek deep holes. Do your fishing early and late in the day there, as well. Work back eddies, around points, and

The aggressive feeding habits of the white bass have earned it the respect of many fly fishers. This one fell for a kiwi muddler.

along drop-offs. Also, look for streams that enter the main river. These smaller creeks often deliver cold, oxygenated water. This attracts both the white bass and their prey species, including minnows and shad.

The best time to target white bass is in the spring, when water temperatures approach the upper 50s. This is when bass in lakes migrate into rivers to spawn and bass in rivers migrate upstream for the same reason. Unlike members of the sunfish family, but like other members of the temperate bass family, white bass do not build nests to protect eggs or fry. This means that angling has nearly no effect on spawning success. If there is a dam in a drainage that contains white bass, be ready for massive schools to congregate directly below it. At the right time, these tailwaters will provide action on every cast.

The Striped Bass

Notes: A favorite saltwater gamefish, the striper is an anadromous fish, meaning that it migrates from the ocean into freshwater rivers to spawn. It has been introduced in many landlocked lakes and reservoirs where it has now become an important freshwater, warmwater gamefish.

Range: Stripers were once native only to the eastern seacoast and the rivers and estuaries connected to the ocean from southern Canada to northern Florida and parts of the Gulf of Mexico. In the late 1800s, they were introduced on the West Coast, where they now range from California to Oregon. Since then, they have been transplanted into many lakes and large impoundments across the southern United States, from California to North Carolina, and they now thrive in the rivers and canals connecting these reservoirs, as well.

Water Types: Lakes, rivers, and canals.

Size: Stripers average 8 pounds, but in areas where food is abundant, particularly in newly created reservoirs where gizzard shad are well established, 20-pounders are commonplace. I grew up on the Massachusetts coast, and have caught many striped bass from the cold New England ocean waters, but ironically, my largest catches, including fish over 30 pounds, came from Elephant Butte Reservoir in New Mexico.

Habitat Preference: Although striped bass are known to enter shallow water to feed, particularly at night, they prefer open water, often as deep as 80 feet. In rivers, they will be found in the deepest holes, and particularly below the dams in tailwaters.

Food Preferences: Foods vary from one locality to another, ranging from any kind of small fish to crustaceans, but a favorite buffet of the landlocked striper is the gizzard shad. Stripers have been known to eat nearly all other fish in a lake or reservoir where they have been introduced.

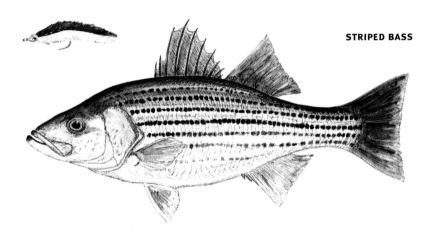

STRIPED BASS

Handling Concerns: Avoid the spines in the dorsal and anal fins. Also be careful of the razor-sharp bone on the gill plates, as well as the jagged gill rakers.

Close Cousins: The white bass, yellow bass, white perch, and "wiper", a hybrid of the striped bass and the white bass.

Recommended Tackle: (based on a 10-pound striped bass).

> **Rod**: 9-foot for an 8-weight line.
>
> **Reel**: These brutes are not your average freshwater quarries. Although a sizzling run is rare, long runs are not. The reel must have a strong, smooth drag and a capacity for 75 to 150 yards of 20-pound backing.
>
> **Line**: 8-weight, weight-forward, intermediate—WF8I—or 8-weight, weight-forward, sinking—WF8S.
>
> **Leader**: Type A, 7 1/2-foot, 15-pound tippet.
>
> **Flies**: The best hook sizes are from 5/0 to 1/0. A favorite color is white, often combined with olive, black, or brown. Excellent patterns include the Sanchez Double Bunny, Lefty's Deceiver, Sanchez's Conehead the Barbarian, Clouser Deep Minnow, Prism Diver Shad, and the Dahlberg Mega Diver.

Tactics

Striped bass are not always easy to locate or catch in fresh water. During the spring, in some places, and during the fall in others, stripers move into rivers to spawn. In many rivers, this means they venture upstream until they arrive at the base of a dam. Naturally, at this dead end they begin to congregate. This predictable calendar event attracts many anglers, because the stripers are easy targets.

In some rivers, however, stripers will remain at the base of dams throughout the year. Water temperatures stay cool enough for them in the summer and warm enough in the winter because water passed through the dam comes from the bottom of the reservoir. Also, food is frequently abundant. Fish such as shad, bass, walleyes, trout, drum, and others, all of which are part of the striper diet, gather here, as well. In some circumstances, fish, particularly gizzard and threadfin shad, get sucked from the reservoir through the dam and into the river. Few can survive the short, harsh trip through the working dam. Those that don't are ground into chunks of body parts and flesh and in turn become chum that is pumped out of the dam, ringing the dinner bell for those ravenous feeders, the waiting stripers.

Fishing for stripers in lakes and reservoirs varies with the season. Surface water temperatures rise during the hot summer months, remaining that way into early fall. Stripers then retreat to depths of over 80 feet. So the time of year to concentrate on stripers with a fly rod in lakes and reservoirs is the spring and late fall, when you are more likely

It's a one way street for the prey of this striped bass.

to find them near the surface. Early mornings and late evenings are good times to encounter them in water shallow enough that you can reach them with a sinking line.

Throughout the night is also effective, because stripers are proficient nocturnal feeders. Cast anywhere that the other fish that stripers eat will seek shelter, such as points, the edges of drop-offs, and over shallow flats. If you have a fish finder, you might even search for schools of suspended baitfish in open water. Stripers are guaranteed to be near. Probe with big flies and scope the water column. Nevertheless, action may be slow and stripers may not be found.

The absolute best fly-fishing opportunities for stripers come when they are feeding on the surface and you can take them on poppers. Look for gulls and terns slamming the water, picking off shad fleeing from attacking stripers beneath. These attacks never last long, because stripers like to return to the depths quickly. That means starting with a popper can be risky because of the limited time before the frenzy ends, but the explosive strike that a surface fly produces makes the risk well worth it. It also means you need to get to the action immediately. Don't spook them with the noise of your motor, though. Let the wind blow you toward them and cast directly into the feeding fury.

Unlike most frenzied fish, feeding stripers can be meticulous and often refuse a fly that isn't the exact size and color of the baitfish on which they are gorging themselves. So I like to have another rod rigged with a streamer, just in case the popper fails. A gray-and-white Sanchez Double Bunny matched exactly to the size of the fleeing shad has the best chance of inducing a strike.

Usually, the fish you will catch are the smaller stripers of the school. These guys are more aggressive than their larger parents, which are often lurking beneath the commotion, feeding with much less effort on sinking chunks of flesh snipped in half and on shad stunned and missed in the hasty attacks going on above. Although it can be difficult, with a heavy fly, you can try to get down deep, past the ferocious smaller schoolies. A trick for doing this is to cast slightly to the side of or across and past the frenzy and simply not strip the fly until it sinks out of sight of the small stripers. Keep a tight grip on the fly line with your stripping hand, though, because there's a good chance that the monsters below will try to rip the line from you while your fly sinks motionless, imitating a tattered hunk of protein.

THE PERCH FAMILY (PERCIDAE)

The perch family consists of hundreds of species worldwide. That's because it includes not only the yellow perch, walleye, and sauger that are valued by most North American anglers, but the darters, a small fish with over one hundred species of its own. The fact that darters are too small for human consumption is why many anglers are not familiar with them.

The perch family does however include several other, larger species that are not found on the North American continent. Europe and Asia share three. The first, the European perch, which is similar to the yellow perch, is the most common and has been transplanted to other parts of the world, including Australia, where it is called the redfin. Also common are the zander, which is similar to the walleye, but grows to a colossal 30 pounds, and the Volga zander, which is likewise similar to the walleye, but does not grow nearly as large as the zander.

All perch are considered a delicacy for the dinner table and are an important sport fish. They all share an enormous appetite for other fish and aquatic insects, and that makes them an easy target for angling. In North America, the yellow perch and the walleye are the best-known members of the perch family and the ones most often pursued. Information I give to help catch these species should apply to their close cousins, as well.

The Yellow Perch

Notes: Classified as a panfish, the yellow perch is the most widely distributed of the perch family. It is a favorite of many anglers who seek fast action and good table fare.

Range: A widespread native of the northern United States and Canada, it has since been stocked in nearly all the southern states, as well.

Water Types: Lakes.

Size: In most regions, the average size is 7 inches. However, where food is plentiful and growing seasons long, the average size can be 10 inches, with 14-inchers not uncommon. I have a jumbo 17-incher from Lake Winnipesaukee, in New Hampshire, hanging on my wall. I caught and stuffed it myself when I was 12.

Habitat Preference: Small yellow perch will live in less than 10 feet of water, hiding under dock pilings and beneath boats, but mature perch will live in depths from 12 to 40 feet. They can tolerate a wide range of water temperatures and water clarity as long as they have some type of structure in which to live, but they thrive in cool, clean water with a mixed bottom of sand, gravel, and boulders.

Food Preferences: Yellow perch eat a wide variety of foods, including minnows and other small fish, crayfish, insects, dragonfly and damselfly nymphs, hellgrammites, snails, and fish eggs.

Handling Concerns: Avoid the spines in the dorsal and anal fins.

Close Cousins: The European Perch.

YELLOW PERCH

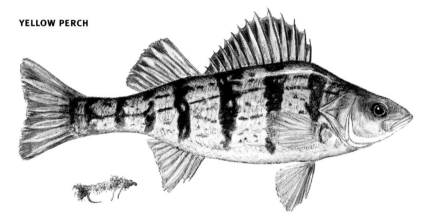

Recommended Tackle: (based on a 10-inch, 3/4-pound yellow perch).

Rod: 9-foot for a 5-weight line.

Reel: Yellow perch are not known for their fighting abilities. The simplest of fly reels will do.

Line: 5-weight, weight-forward, floating—WF5F—or 5-weight, weight-forward, sinking—WF5S.

Leader: Type A, 9-foot, 4-pound to 6-pound tippet.

Flies: The best hook sizes are from 6 to 10. I have caught yellow perch on flies of nearly every imaginable color, but my first choices are black, olive, and brown, the colors of much of their natural prey. Excellent patterns include the Woolly Bugger, Conehead Mohair Leech, Beadhead Kaufmann Rubber-Leg Stone, Sanchez Damsel Nymph, Dave's Hopper, and the Sanchez Crawdaddy.

Tactics

During the spring, about one month after ice-out, was by far the best time to seek yellow perch in my home waters in New Hampshire. Preparing to spawn, large schools gathered within casting range of our boat dock. Any concoction of a lure or fly, tossed to where the shallows dropped off and retrieved quickly or slowly, would send the entire perch school into a frenzy. Literally every perch that saw the fly, sometimes over a hundred, would charge to it as if it were the equivalent of a hot fudge sundae to an ice-cream freak. Not only I, but also my brother and sister and several cousins, would connect with these cooperative fish for hours on end.

Though yellow perch populations have diminished around our family dock over the last 20 years, in many regions, great early season action continues to flourish. If you're fortunate enough to hit a blitz like this, use up the oldest, rattiest, flies in your box, because it is not beauty that these aggressive fish require.

When spawning ends and water temperatures begin to rise, the challenge of fly fishing for yellow perch begins. These enormous and seemingly suicidal schools of perch break into smaller groups, often according to size, and retreat to deeper, cooler water. There they spend the remainder of the summer, feeding on minnows, crayfish, and varieties of aquatic insects. If you know the locations of drop-offs, large boulders, or brush piles in 15 to 40 feet of water, you're in business. Such locations will produce perch throughout the season. Although the fish are not quite as aggressive as in the early spring, streamers and nymphs towed deep behind fast-sinking lines in these locations will produce strikes.

My favorite method of fly fishing for yellow perch is to pursue them before sunrise on a cool summer morning. It is an excellent time to catch them on the surface. Like most warmwater species, perch are opportunistic feeders and will look for an easy meal. Foods include hatched insects such as mayflies, caddis, dragonflies, damselflies, and stoneflies, as well as drowned terrestrial insects such as grasshoppers, cicadas, crickets, ants, and beetles. Like trout gulping mayflies from the surface on a Rocky Mountain lake, perch cruise and search for these drifting snacks. Look for gentle dimples on the surface. When you spot a fish, study the situation carefully. Note the distance between rises, and more importantly, identify the direction in which the feeding fish is headed. You must get the fly in the fish's path. Gingerly presented dry flies on long leaders will fool these wary, surface-feeding perch.

The Walleye (Walleyed Pike, Pike-Perch)

Notes: Although the walleye has a poor reputation for fighting abilities, it is a favorite sport fish. Its delicious, sweet meat makes it the best table fare of all the freshwater fish, and its unique, large, white reflective eyes make the walleye mysteriously attractive to any angler.

Range: Native to the Northern United States and much of Canada. It has since been introduced as far south as South Carolina and westward to Arizona.

Water Types: Lakes and rivers.

Size: Commonly reaches 14 to 19 inches, or about 1 to 3 pounds. A 6-pounder deserves recognition, although this large member of the perch family can reach 20 pounds.

Habitat Preference: Water from 4 to 30 feet in depth. Most feeding, however, is done at depths of less than 20 feet. Walleyes prefer cool, unmuddied water with both gravel and sandy bottoms, but will forage around weeds, sunken trees, brush piles, and wherever they may find minnows to eat.

Food Preferences: The walleye's primary diet is small fish and minnows, but it also loves leeches and crayfish.

Handling Concerns: Avoid the spines in the dorsal and anal fins and take care around the needlelike teeth and sharp gill covers.

Close Cousins: The sauger and the zander of Europe and Asia.

Recommended Tackle: (based on a 19-inch, 2-pound walleye).

> **Rod:** 9-foot for a 6-weight line.
>
> **Reel:** Even a big walleye gives only a short struggle as you bring it up off the bottom. But a smooth drag, rather than a jerky one, could save a tippet from being severed on a walleye's razor-sharp teeth.

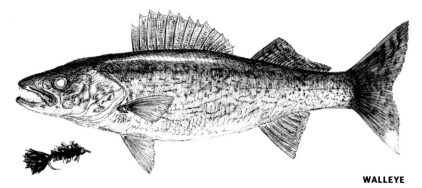

WALLEYE

Line: 6-weight, weight-forward, sinking—WF6S.
Leader: Type A, 9-foot, 6-pound to 8-pound tippet.
Flies: The best hook sizes are from 2 to 6. My first color choice is black. However, fluorescent colors like chartreuse, orange, red, and yellow are also effective. Stick entirely to wet flies such as the Clouser Deep Minnow, Sanchez's Conehead the Barbarian, Woolly Bugger, Conehead Mohair Leech, Beadhead Rubber-Leg Kaufmann Stone, and the Sanchez Crawdaddy.

Tactics

The walleye is one of the more cunning of the warmwater species. Anglers who understand the habits of these fish catch them regularly, while those who don't catch them only by accident. They are quick to refuse live bait solely because it's not hooked correctly. In addition, they have a mouthful of sharp teeth and an abrasive gill plate that can shave through a 6-pound-test tippet in seconds, yet if you fish a tippet heavier than 8-pound-test, you may not get a strike at all.

In a lake, walleyes typically spend most of their day resting on bottom in 20 to 30 feet of water, usually just over the edge of a shelf or drop-off in close proximity to a shallow hump, reef, or sandbar. Although dredging these areas by day will produce the occasional random walleye, it is generally unproductive because walleyes are nocturnal feeders. The minute the sun drops below the horizon, however, walleyes awake and charge to the shallows in schools. If you catch one, you will likely catch more from the same area.

When I was a hard-core Wisconsin ice fisherman, I never hit the lake before three in the afternoon when seeking walleyes. I set my tip-ups, which take the place of a rod in ice fishing, over an area ranging from about 6 to 14 feet deep on an undulating gravel shoal near the edge of a drop-off. The regulations allowed the use of 3 lines per angler, so a group of friends typically had 12 tip-ups scattered across the ice and baited with live fathead minnows. From four until five, we would sporadically catch a walleye or two, but after five, when the sun dropped, the flags on our tip-ups would pop. I can remember one incredible night when all 12 tip-ups were triggered within minutes after sunset.

The type of bottom over which walleyes prefer to hunt has less structure than what other warmwater species normally favor. They prefer undulating bottoms with gravel and sandbars with just an occasional boulder or brush pile or a scattering of weeds, simply enough

Small yellow perch are dinner for big walleye, but this perch is safe because the sleeping walleye isn't much bigger than he.

cover to attract minnows, leeches, and crayfish. A slight chop on the water (often called a walleye chop in the Midwest) not only hides the angler from cruising walleyes in the shallows, but allows for the productive method of drifting with the wind in a boat while dredging leech patterns on sinking lines and bouncing the bottom with coneheads and Clouser Deep Minnows.

Spring is a particularly good time to fly fish for walleyes on rivers. Walleyes spawn at this time, and as they roam upstream in search of ideal habitat to deposit and fertilize their eggs, like many other species, they often reach a dead end at a dam. Most states close fishing for walleyes at this time, or at least at these locations, but both before the season closes and after opening day, the fish may be found in the swirling currents below a dam, providing an excellent opportunity to catch them. When your timing is right, it's not uncommon to catch these often wary fish one after another.

Soon after they spawn, walleyes become challenging fish to catch. They disperse to other portions of the river or back to the lake. In rivers, concentrate on the deepest holes. Daytime fishing can be productive on rivers if you can get your fly down deep, but current makes it difficult to reach the river's bottom, where they are feeding. When this is the case, wait until sunset and work the shallows. Gravel points, the edges of islands, shallow inside turns, and riprap all attract minnows and in turn become favorite haunts for walleyes.

When walleyes feed in shallow water, they make an ideal fly-rod quarry. The fact that they prefer lightly structured areas make it easy for bouncing a weighted fly along the bottom through the walleyes' feeding grounds, snag-free. The most important thing to remember when fly fishing for walleyes is to concentrate your efforts after sunset and keep your flies close to the bottom.

A tiger muskie waits motionless for a passing meal.

THE PIKE FAMILY (ESOCIDAE)

The members of the pike family are highly regarded gamefish found throughout the Northern Hemisphere. They willingly take flies, and the larger species are popular for their strong fighting abilities. The group consists of five species: the redfin pickerel, grass pickerel, chain pickerel, northern pike, and muskellunge. There is also the "tiger muskie", a sterile hybrid of the pike and the muskellunge. The chain pickerel, northern pike, and muskellunge are the best-known members of the pike family and the ones most often pursued. Information I give to help catch these species should apply to their close cousins, as well.

The Chain Pickerel (Jackfish or Pike)

Notes: The chain pickerel is rarely targeted and is unappreciated by most anglers. However, they take top-water flies well and on light fly tackle can put up a respectable fight.

Range: Native from eastern Texas to Florida and northward to New England. It can be found toward the Great Lakes, but rarely coexists with larger members of the pike family, which dominate in these areas.

Water Types: Ponds, lakes, rivers, and canals.
Size: Commonly reaches 16 inches, but 19-inchers are not infrequent. In the southern reaches of its range, pickerel over 25 inches are not unheard of, with some mammoth catches exceeing 30 inches and over 8 pounds.

CHAIN PICKEREL

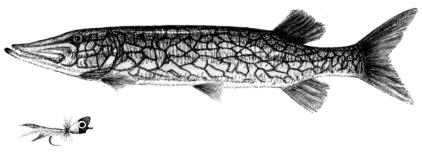

Habitat Preference: Water from shore to 10 feet deep. Pickerel thrive in weedy areas. However, occasionally, large pickerel live around docks or inside boathouses.
Food Preferences: Mainly other fish, including their own kind, but crayfish, frogs, mice, salamanders, insects, and other small mouthfuls that venture too close during dinner time are likely victims.
Handling Concerns: Beware of their sharp, needlelike teeth. Always remove the fly with pliers.
Close Cousins: The redfin pickerel, grass pickerel, and northern pike.
Recommended Tackle: (based on a 16-inch, 1-pound chain pickerel).
   Rod: 9-foot for a 5-weight line.
   Reel: Pickerel put up a nice struggle on light tackle, but long runs do not occur. A basic reel with a single-pawl or dual-pawl drag system is sufficient.
   Line: 5-weight, weight-forward, floating—WF5F.
   Leader: Type A, 7 1/2-foot, 6-pound to 8-pound tippet.
   Flies: The best sizes are from 4 to 10. Pickerel love bright, sunny days. Therefore I use flies tied with bright colors. Excellent patterns include the Standard Popper, Prism Diver, Mouserat, Swimming Frog, Sanchez Double Bunny, and Clouser Deep Minnow.

Tactics

Small freshwater versions of barracuda, chain pickerel sit motionless in the shallows, camouflaged as sticks as they wait for the unaware victim to venture too close. On a good day of fly fishing, that victim should be your fly, but these small members of the pike family can be trickier to catch than you might think. One day you may swear there are no pickerel in the water you're fishing, while the next day in the exact same place, you may hook many.

I regularly pursue chain pickerel with top-water flies. Streamers work, especially a red-and-white Clouser Deep Minnow or a conehead pattern, both of which have jigging movement, but because pickerel thrive in shallow, weedy areas, subsurface fishing can mean frustrating snags, one after another. Small Prism Divers or frog or mouse patterns slid across a quiet pond surface work well where big pickerel lurk, but it is the Standard Popper, about a size 8, that always seems to produce a strike from a pickerel.

Since pickerel prefer to wait for meals to come to them, begin by blind casting to specific likely holding spots. Narrow gaps between weed beds, open areas among a vast spread of lily pads, protruding logs, or shady dock edges are good places to try. I particularly like to fish just off the fringe of a beach or boat launch where there often is a 6-foot infertile area before thick weeds begin to grow. On a river, work all the grassy sloughs and other out-of-the-way nooks and crannies. Any of these places allows a pickerel several feet of viewing to spot and spring on unsuspecting prey.

This chain pickerel mistook the standard popper for a frog.

Unlike bass or crappies, which favor long hesitations between pops of a popper, pickerel prefer a more steady popping action. Cast as far as you can and begin a retrieve of uniform strips 6 inches long. Watch for V-shaped wakes angling toward your fly. An oncoming pickerel is swimming near the surface. When you see one approaching, you have an interested customer.

Sometimes the wake never stops charging the fly, and you'll get an immediate strike, but if not, whatever you do, don't slow your retrieve. Wary pickerel, perhaps because they have been previously hooked or are alert to your presence, may want to follow and examine your fly from an inch behind its tail. If you have room to continue retrieving before the leader meets the rod tip, keep stripping at the same speed that attracted the pickerel in the first place. If the pickerel follows another few feet and doesn't strike or turns away, pick up the pace. Turn those 6-inch strips into foot-long jerks. This makes it harder for the pickerel to examine your fly.

If you run out of room, and the leader meets the rod tip, don't give up yet. Simply swish the fly from side to side in a figure-eight motion. I have had pickerel eat the fly right before my eyes, sometimes even as I pull the fly out of the water. If all these ruses fail, and the pickerel vanishes, chances are you won't see it again that day. However, pickerel are territorial, so if you miss out on a lunker one day, remember the location and try again on another.

The Northern Pike (Pike, Northern, Great Northern Pike, or Water Wolf)

Notes: A ferocious predator! Northern pike are common within their range, grow large, and fight excellently. They take artificial baits well and are a popular gamefish.

Range: Native not only throughout the northern regions of North America, but also in Europe and Asia. In Canada, pike are found nearly everywhere east of the Rocky Mountains except in the extreme Arctic regions. Their range extends south into the northern United States throughout the Great Lakes region, east to New York, and west to the Rocky Mountains. They have since been stocked throughout the Rocky Mountain states.

Water Types: Lakes and rivers.

Habitat Preference: Water from 6 to 20 feet deep. Pike like structure, particularly weeds, scattered brush, and logs.

NORTHERN PIKE

Size: Commonly reaches 30 inches and over 7 pounds, but in many regions, pike regularly exceed 12 pounds. With the exception of remote Canadian waters, 20-pounders are rare, however monsters over 40 pounds have been recorded.

Food Preferences: Any trespasser smaller than itself is supper. Minnows, sunfish, perch, walleyes, chubs, and young muskies are regular menu items. Pike even seem to enjoy feasting on their own kind. Ducklings, mice, voles, shrews, and muskrats must swim in fear at all times.

Handling Concerns: Beware of razor-sharp, fanglike teeth. Always remove your fly with needle-nosed pliers.

Close Cousins: The tiger muskie, muskellunge, and the chain pickerel.

Recommended Tackle: (based on a 30-inch, 7-pound pike).

> **Rod:** 9-foot for an 8-weight line.
>
> **Reel:** A 7-pound pike is a lot of fish. It will pull hard, often in sporadic surges. Although backing-stealing runs aren't common, I have 75 yards attached to a reel with a strong, smooth drag.
>
> **Line:** 7-weight, weight-forward, floating—WF7F—or any of the fly lines specifically designed for pike.
>
> **Leader:** Type C leader, 7 1/2-foot, 12-pound class tippet and 40-pound wire tippet.
>
> **Flies:** The best hook sizes are from 3/0 to 2. Favorite colors are white, chartreuse, and red and white combined. Excellent patterns include the Dahlberg Mega Diver, Prism Diver, Swimming Frog, Mouserat, Sanchez Double Bunny, and Lefty's Deceiver.

Tactics

Undoubtedly, spring is the best time of year to pursue northern pike with a fly rod. This is when pike, which prefer cooler water than their cousins, are commonly found in the shallows, both to spawn and to enjoy cool, but not freezing water temperatures after spending the winter under as much as 3 feet of ice. During these perfect conditions, they are not only remarkably aggressive, eating nearly every moving object smaller than themselves, but also easy to reach with gigantic surface flies attached to a wire bite tippet and a floating line.

Not all shallow areas on a lake will support pike. Northerns usually select bays that have dark, muddy bottoms. These areas tend to heat up faster than areas with light, sandy bottoms and also harbor many aquatic weeds, from cattails to lily pads, habitat in which pike thrive.

A 10-pound pike has no problem patiently awaiting prey in a mere foot of water, but when doing so, it will practically always be surrounded by a fortress of structure. Most often, these will be reeds, cattails, grass, or some other form of aquatic vegetation, but could be brush or fallen trees, as well. Therefore, it is almost required that you begin with a weedless top-water fly.

An enormous Standard Popper is a great fly choice. Pike home in quickly on the noisy, gurgling sound it makes. If you're in pike-infested waters, it is not uncommon to have two wakes racing through the shallows to get a piece of the intruding artificial on the first cast. Only on rare occasions does a pike turn away during the pursuit of the fly. However, I have had it happen and believe that it may be because I popped the fly too hard just when a pike was going to make the kill, perhaps startling it. Conceivably, it could be a pike that has previously been hooked, or perhaps it has been injured recently by struggling prey. I recommend that you go back to the spot later and use a fly that pops more gently and dives deeper. Both the Prism Diver and the Mega Diver pop gently, dive, and slowly rise back to the surface. Watch as the northern hammers the fly between pops, as it rises.

In the far north, pike may remain in shallow water throughout the short summer season, but in most regions, northerns retreat to slightly deeper water. When they do, concentrate your fishing near drop-offs and channels and especially the necks of bays, where pike were found during the spring. Although the top-water action isn't altogether over, streamers dropped down to the pike's haunts with sinking lines will produce jolting strikes. Traditionally, the first choice of spin-fishing anglers to fool pike down deep is a red-and-white Daredevil. This color combination has been proven for decades. Thus, a big fly in red and white is my first choice. A Lefty's Deceiver, a popular saltwater streamer, is a deadly match.

Slow, wide, meandering rivers overflowing onto adjacent land, often referred to as flowages, can offer unique pike fisheries. Muskie anglers in Wisconsin frequently search the sloughs and deep, lakelike areas for this elusive giant, only to catch plenty of pike. Trout anglers on the Flathead River in Montana and the Yampa River in Colorado reach with the net to snare the gorgeous rainbows of these streams, only to have them plucked from their leaders and devoured in an instant by hungry northerns. On the Yampa, this is especially common. Therefore, many fly fishers specifically target pike. Because they are under more fishing pressure than their Canadian relatives, the pike of the Yampa are somewhat shy, frequently following, then refusing flies presented on Type C leaders with wire bite tippets. When they do, I fish a Type B leader with a 12-pound class tippet attached to a heavy, 30-pound mono shock tippet, which is just invisible enough to the northern to increase the frequency of strikes considerably, yet strong enough to land most of the fish. In the backwaters of this unique river, top-water flies will take pike, but Lefty's Deceivers produce regularly, even in the main river channel.

The Muskellunge (Muskie)

Notes: A fine gamefish because of its size and strength. However, it is perhaps the most difficult of all freshwater species to catch. The habits of this great fish have never been fully understood.

Range: Unlike the northern pike, the muskellunge is found only in North America. It is native throughout the Great Lakes and east to New York, and from southern Quebec to Manitoba. It has been introduced farther south, particularly in the Atlantic states as far south as North Carolina.

Water Types: Rivers and lakes.

Size: The largest member of the pike family, muskies have been caught up to 69 pounds, however in the 1990s, very few fish over 40 pounds tipped the scales. Today, an average muskie weighs 10 pounds, and one over 20 pounds is a dandy catch.

Habitat Preference: During the spring, or when the water is cold, muskies are found in depths of from 5 to 15 feet. During the summer, they move to water as much as 25 feet deep.

Food Preferences: Any fish half the size of the muskie itself is fair prey. Northern pike, walleyes, yellow perch, bass, trout, chubs, shiners, and suckers are favorites, although frogs, turtles, snakes, newts, small ducks, mice, voles, shrews, and muskrats are regularly dined upon.

Handling Concerns: Beware of the razor-sharp, fanglike teeth. Always remove your fly with needle-nosed pliers.

Close Cousins: The tiger muskie and the northern pike.

Recommended Tackle: (based on a 46-inch, 20-pound muskellunge).

Rod: 9-foot for a 9-weight line.

Reel: Any time you specifically target muskies, you'd better be prepared for that once-in-a-lifetime monster! A reel with a strong, smooth drag is an absolute requirement to absorb sudden surges and erratic head thrashes. Capacity for 75 yards of 20-pound backing is sufficient.

Line: 9-weight, weight-forward, floating—WF9F—or any fly line specifically designed for pike and muskie.

Leader: Type C, 7 1/2-foot, 12-pound class tippet and 40-pound wire shock tippet.

Flies: The best hook sizes are from 3/0 to 2. The muskie's favorite colors are ones that match its prey, such as brown, olive, gray, and black, yet the combination of red and white has proven itself for many years. Excellent patterns include the Dahlberg Mega Diver, Prism Diver, Swimming Frog, Mouserat, Sanchez Double Bunny, and Lefty's Deceiver.

MUSKELLUNGE

Tactics

The muskellunge may be the most humbling of all freshwater game-fish. In most parts of its range, it is either rare or uncommon. Where it does thrive, anglers who consistently pursue muskies may go years before actually seeing one, because they are the wiliest of all North American gamefish, and are unpredictable and inscrutable in their ways. When a big muskie finally strikes, the fish still often defeats the angler. The hook must be razor-sharp in order to penetrate the rock-hard, tooth-filled mouth. Then, if you are fortunate enough to hook one, the muskie's robust fighting ability makes for slim odds of landing it.

It takes a dedicated fly fisher to chase muskies. Over a period of 4 years while living in northern Wisconsin, I made regular trips to the Chippewa Flowage, not only the heart of muskie territory, but home of the 69-pound, 11-ounce world record. I used both a spinning rod and fly rod during my quest. After well over an estimated 200 hours worth of targeting muskies, I had zero follows on the fly and zero strikes on favorite muskie lures. I did, however, have one eat a 14-inch live sucker, which I am ashamed to say I dangled below a softball-sized red-and-white bobber in total desperation.

Despite my dishonorable method, the moment that oversized bobber slowly submerged was one of the greatest adrenaline rushes I've had in my fishing career. After a torturous 45 minutes, seemingly longer than any hour-long high school history lesson, which is the time it usually takes for a muskie to position and swallow a sucker, I set the hook with an incredible thrust with my heavy-action spinning rod. To my pleasure, the weight of what turned out to be a mammoth muskie was there, but the fight was not. In a state of disbelief, I simply reeled the monster to within sight of the boat. There, just out of reach of our long-handled net with a hoop large enough to snare a tarpon, the monster stopped my tackle dead in its tracks. Raising its long nose with a look of disgust, it reluctantly let go of the sucker and with a flip of its shovel-length body vanished into the dark water. Though heartbroken, my friend and I felt some degree of success from having achieved the mere glimpse of this great fish.

Nearly twenty years have passed since that day. Ironically, I now look back on my close encounter and can honestly say I am glad the big muskie escaped. That's because I would have undoubtedly kept the fish. I have since netted muskies from those same pristine Wisconsin waters. Actually to hold one of these special creatures makes you appreciate the need to maintain their existence. The practice of catch-and-release fishing is crucial.

There are some exceptions to the difficulty involved in catching a muskie. In some areas, they are abundant, and small individuals are caught with regularity. These fish offer great fly-fishing opportunities. Cast the biggest fly you can, and more importantly, be persistent. Casting for 30 minutes and resting is not the way to fool a muskie. It takes hours upon hours with the fly in the water.

Even in the best locations, where there's a good chance the fish are actually there when you cast your fly, catching these elusive giants isn't easy, but with some basic knowledge of where to look for them, your chances will increase. As when targeting most fish, search areas with vegetation, particularly where weeds end, meeting deeper water. Cast to submerged islands bordered by deep water, basically places that attract walleyes and yellow perch. Inlets where rivers pour in and power-plant discharges on a lake are worthy places to try. In rivers themselves, sloughs, backwaters, and any deep pool will hold muskies. When a muskie is located, remember that spot. Muskies have territories and seldom roam.

When you are confident a muskie is present, work an area diligently. Muskies are rarely first-cast fish. Although top-water flies work, begin with a streamer. Muskies love a big, hearty meal, so a Lefty's Deceiver or a Double Bunny 6 to 8 inches long, if you can cast a fly that big, has as good a chance as any fly. The standard combination of red and white is a good first choice, but be prepared to change flies. Custom ties that resemble a yellow perch or a sucker are about as realistic as you can get. Present them first with a floating line, but don't leave the area until you have dredged the depths of a hole with a sinking line. Mentally prepare yourself to understand that just sighting a muskie behind your fly makes for a somewhat successful day.

The Tiger Muskie (Norlunge)

Combine what you have learned about the northern pike and the muskellunge and you will have what it takes to catch a tiger muskie. Although tigers do occur naturally, they are commonly the result of the deliberate crossbreeding of pike and muskies in hatcheries. The tiger muskie has become a popular gamefish because it grows quickly and eats aggressively, like a pike, but looks more like a muskellunge. These are a beautifully marked fish and have been introduced to many areas where neither of their parent species exists.

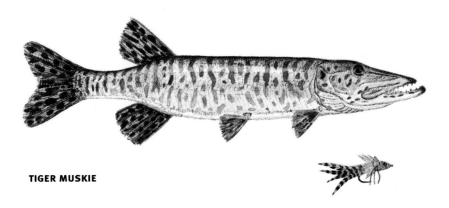

TIGER MUSKIE

THE CATFISH FAMILY (ICTALURIDAE)

Barbels around their broad, flattened heads easily distinguish the catfish family. They are bottom dwellers, nocturnal hunters with poor eyesight that typically feed by feel and smell and therefore are caught most regularly by anglers using bait. However, like most fish, they are opportunists that, when given an opportunity, will lash out with an aggressive strike to subdue an easy meal in the form of a slow-moving baitfish, leech, or crayfish. So when presented with an artificial lure or fly at close range, they will often strike.

Although most anglers simply refer to any catfish as a catfish, there are many different species found throughout the world. The North American species important to angling include the blue catfish, white catfish, channel catfish, flathead catfish, yellow bullhead, brown bullhead, and black bullhead.

Channel catfish are probably the most commonly caught catfish on artificial baits, and I'll focus on them here. Catches usually occur when chasing other bottom-dwelling species such as walleyes, perch, or drum. Several years ago, for example, while fishing a Double Bunny for striped bass, I landed a 9-pound, 12-ounce channel cat. After I submitted photos and certified the scale on which I weighed this obese cat, it was later recognized by the National Fresh Water Fishing Hall of Fame as the catch-and-release fly-rod world record for the 12-pound tippet class. It was a very unexpected thrill added to what had already been a phenomenal day of striper fishing. But it is possible to target channel cats deliberately when fishing with a fly rod.

The author releases a 9-pound 12-ounce National Freshwater Hall of Fame World Record channel catfish for the 12-pound tippet class. New Mexico's Elephant Butte Reservoir – 1993.

The Channel Catfish (Channel Cat)

Notes: The most widely distributed of North America's freshwater catfish and ranked highly by most anglers because it is easy to catch and has delicious flesh.

Range: Native from the Rocky Mountains east to the Appalachians and from southern Canada to northeastern Mexico. Channel cats have since been introduced in the waters of both the West Coast and the East Coast of North America.

Water Types: Ponds, lakes, rivers, and canals.

Size: Commonly reaches 2 to 5 pounds. Fish exceeding 15 pounds are infrequent, and any catch over 20 pounds deserves special recognition.

Habitat Preference: In the clear waters of slow-moving rivers and the still waters of lakes and ponds, depths from 3 to 25 feet. They prefer bottoms with areas of sand and gravel and with occasional boulders, drop-offs, or any structure that creates a crevice that not only provides shelter from daylight, but also attracts minnows on which to feed.

Food Preferences: Some vegetation, minnows and other small fish such as sunfish, plus fish eggs, crayfish, insects, and the carcasses of larger fish.

Handling Concerns: Avoid the spines, not only in the dorsal fin, but also in the pectorals. Venomous glands in these spines make the wounds they inflict doubly painful.

Close Cousins: The blue catfish, white catfish, flathead catfish, yellow bullhead, brown bullhead, and black bullhead.

Recommended Tackle: (based on a 5-pound channel catfish).

> **Rod:** 9-foot for a 7-weight line.
>
> **Reel:** Bulldogging head shakes will occur, but long runs will not. A reel with a smooth drag won't hurt.
>
> **Line:** 7-weight, weight-forward, sinking—WF7S.
>
> **Leader:** Type A, 7 1/2-foot, 8-pound to 12-pound tippet.
>
> **Flies:** The best hook sizes are from 1/0 to 4. Catfish have poor eyesight, so bright colors should be used during the day. At night, use black to cast the best silhouette. Excellent patterns include the Clouser Deep Minnow, Sanchez's Conehead the Barbarian, Whitlock's Softshell Crayfish, the Sanchez Double Bunny, Conehead Mohair Leech, and the Beadhead Rubber-Leg Kaufmann Stone.

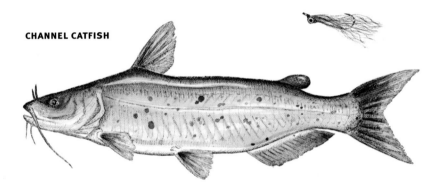

CHANNEL CATFISH

Tactics

Although catfish are attracted to the smell of many foods, they will eat a fly stripped slowly, directly in front of them. In fact, if you can literally nick a whisker (a barbel), they will often aggressively attack the fly in annoyance. On a city pond where people feed ducks, it is not uncommon for schools of channel cats to linger, suspended, feeding on sinking bread scraps. A similar situation occurs on private ponds and lakes where owners feed carp and bream, as well as in areas where filleted fish carcasses have been disposed of in the water.

Although channel cats are caught under these unique daytime circumstances, night fishing with bottom-bouncing flies stripped through areas where channel cats are common also will produce results.

Dock lights that attract insects and the fish that eat them also bring in curious cats. Just as you would during the day, make an accurate cast and strip the fly right in front of the cat.

THE DRUM FAMILY (SCIAENIDAE)

The drum family includes mostly saltwater species, such as the red drum and the black drum, both of which are important gamefish along the North American coasts, commonly in the brackish water of river mouths and estuaries. There is, however, one strictly freshwater species, the freshwater drum.

The Freshwater Drum (Sheepshead or Thunder-Pumper)

Notes: An extremely underutilized freshwater species, usually caught only accidentally while seeking more popular gamefish.

Range: Native east of the Rocky Mountains to the Appalachian Mountains and from Manitoba to Mexico.

Water Types: Lakes and rivers.

Size: Commonly reaches 16 inches and 3 pounds, but 20-inchers over 5 pounds are taken regularly. Mammoth catches exceeding 50 pounds have been recorded.

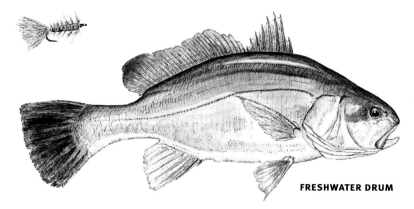

FRESHWATER DRUM

Habitat Preference: Water from 6 to 40 feet deep. Freshwater drum prefer clear water, but can withstand murky water without difficulty.

Food Preferences: Freshwater clams and mussels, aquatic insects, crayfish, leeches, and minnows.

Handling Concerns: Avoid the spines in the dorsal and anal fins. Also beware of the crushers in the back of the throat, which are used for crushing and opening shells.

Close Cousins: The saltwater black drum.
Recommended Tackle: (based on a 16-inch, 3-pound freshwater drum).
> **Rod:** 9-foot for a 7-weight line.
> **Reel:** Big drum are strong fighters, but long runs do not typically occur. A reel with a smooth drag will be sufficient.
> **Line:** 7-weight, weight-forward, sinking—WF7S.
> **Leader:** Type A, 9-foot, 10-pound tippet.
> **Flies:** The best hook sizes are from 2 to 6. Dull colors work best—olive, rust, brown—but bright colors have caught many drum unintentionally. Excellent patterns include Whitlock's Softshell Crayfish, the Woolly Bugger, Conehead Mohair Leech, Beadhead Rubber-Leg Hare's Ear, Beadhead Rubber-Leg Kaufmann Stone, Sanchez Damsel Nymph, and the Clouser Deep Minnow.

Tactics

Many fly fishers who seek popular warmwater species such as bass, perch, and pike with a fly rod have at one time or another caught and landed a freshwater drum. Usually after a nonchalant release and immediate return to the pursuit of a more admired species, they forget about the accidental catch of the less glorious adversary. However, if they were to look back on the respectable battle that occurred, they might think, "Let's try for another one," and if they did, they might find that this neglected species can be challenging and rewarding to catch.

Drum are best pursued during the summer months, when water temperatures are highest. Although they thrive in lakes and reservoirs, these vast areas make them difficult to find for more than an occasional catch. Rivers, on the other hand, offer better chances for flyrodders to find and catch these fish.

Like many species, drum often congregate in the pool nearest to the base of a dam. If you find one there, you likely find many more and can be in for hours of fun, but you must get your fly down to them. Drum are for the most part bottom feeders and will rarely eat a fly that is not within inches of their natural prey's habitat. Undoubtedly, the best way to do this is with a heavy fly such as a Clouser Deep Minnow. A Clouser stripped slowly, with an added lift and drop with the rod tip, will cover the bottom well, likely bumping right into many of the schooling drum. In an especially deep pool, use a sinking fly line, but in less then 10 feet of water, a floating line should be sufficient. In fact, many strikes will occur between strips and lifts, and if you watch the floating fly line's tip carefully, you may see it jerk forward. Essentially, it is a strike indicator.

There are times, however, when you must search for drum in other holding areas and fish for them patiently with different flies and varied stripping techniques. Search for drop-offs, typically below riffles or sand-bars, or where smaller creeks join a river, places with deeper pools and slower-moving current. Not only do these support freshwater clams and mussels, favorite foods for the drum, but they are also locations where minnows, leeches, and crayfish collect to avoid fighting swift currents.

Freshwater drum are fun to catch on a fly.

If there's a heavy concentration of mollusks, you can almost guarantee that's what the drum are feeding on. Since it's difficult to fish a fly that imitates a freshwater mussel or snail, both animals that barely move, you have to fish a streamer or nymph of some sort. Realize that drum are unlikely to waste energy chasing a scurrying bug or fleeing minnow and use short strips, an inch at a time, with long pauses in between. Moving the fly slowly is also important when water temperatures are cool, because the metabolism of these fish, which prefer warm water, will be slowed.

When mollusks are scarce, drum will be feeding on whatever they can find. Sculpins or darters, bottom-dwelling baitfish, as well as cray-fish and leeches, become the drum's regular diet. This is when a foot-long strip and a pause just long enough for a fly to sink back to the bottom will nail fish consistently. Sometimes the fly doesn't even need to sink to the bottom. In Lake Ontario, where there has been a popu-lation explosion of freshwater drum over the last few years, they are caught with regularity on flies stripped at all levels throughout the water column. These fish feed almost entirely on shiners and alewives.

THE MINNOW FAMILY (CYPRINIDAE)

The minnow family is one of the largest families of freshwater fishes. They are important because their abundance and size make them valuable food sources to other fish. Despite the fact that most are too small to consider for angling, there are several species that grow large enough to be taken on fly tackle. Many species of chub, squawfish, goldfish, and shiner are caught while in pursuit of other gamefish, but the carp, the largest member of the family, is often sought in its own right.

The common carp (sometimes called the scaled carp), an exotic from Asia and Europe that thrives in North America, not only lives in pristine lakes and rivers, but also in the ponds of metropolitan centers, making it the most popular of all carp. Two other varieties can be found as well, the mirror carp and the leather carp. The mirror carp, rare in North America, has three rows of huge scales, one along its back, another laterally, and a row along the belly. The leather carp is scaleless and found only in Europe and Asia. There is also the grass carp, or white amur, a carp different from the varieties of common carp. It has the same large scales, but does not have the suckerlike mouth of the common carp. It, too, is an exotic from Asia and was brought to North America because of its eating habits. It eats vegetation and therefore helps reduce excessive amounts in ponds and lakes. The grass carp can be taken on a seed or vegetation-imitating fly.

Few fly fishers search for squawfish, but if they will munch on these dace they will certainly eat a Sanchez Double Bunny.

The Common Carp (The Golden Bonefish)

Notes: This popular and highly regarded fish in Europe and Asia is disrespected in North America and considered a trash fish. However, as catch-and-release sport fishing grows in popularity, so does the pursuit of carp. They are hefty fish that put up a magnificent battle on any tackle.

Range: Native to Europe and Asia, the common carp has been introduced throughout the world, including North America, Africa, Australia, New Zealand, and the United Kingdom. It is found in nearly every U.S. state.

Water Types: Ponds, lakes, rivers, and canals.

Size: Commonly reaches 15 to 25 pounds, and 40-pounders are not uncommon. Record catches have exceeded 60 pounds.

Habitat Preference: Carp can adapt to nearly any habitat except extremely cold water. They prefer water 3 to 6 feet deep and particularly like soft bottoms that are rich in vegetation.

Food Preferences: Vegetation, insect larvae, minnows, fish eggs, snails, tiny freshwater clams, crayfish, freshwater shrimp, bird droppings, and surface-floating seeds and insects. Carp selectively scrounge for a variety of different foods.

Handling Concerns: Other than the fact that a huge carp will slime you to death, be careful with carp. Large carp cannot support their massive body weight out of the water. Don't pick them up by the mouth or the gills, because they will literally tear apart.

Close Cousins: The mirror carp, leather carp, grass carp, and some members of the sucker family.

Recommended Tackle: (based on a 12-pound common carp).

Rod: 9-foot for an 8-weight line.

Reel: Carp over 10 pounds will test any reel. It must have not only a strong, smooth drag, but also capacity for at least 75 yards of 20-pound backing.

Line: 8-weight, weight-forward, floating—WF8F.

Leader: Type A, 9-foot, 8-pound to 12-pound tippet.

Flies: The best hook sizes are from 4 to 18. Your fly should be the color of the natural bait or creature you are imitating. Excellent patterns include Sanchez's Damsel Nymph, the Beadhead Rubber-Leg Hare's Ear, Beadhead Rubber-Leg Kaufmann Stone, Woolly Bugger, Sanchez Crawdaddy, Dave's Hopper, and the Chernobyl Ant.

COMMON CARP

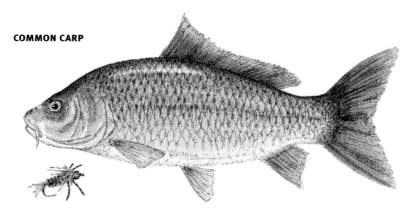

Tactics

Most trout fly fishers turn up their noses at the thought of pursuing a common carp on a fly rod. But this often disrespected fish is perhaps the spookiest of all freshwater species, which means that stalking them can be challenging and exciting. Carp also can reach huge sizes, can be sight fished like bonefish, fight tremendously hard, and are as difficult to fool into eating a fly as even the most selective trout. Best of all, they are abundant nearly everywhere. The common carp is worthy of special attention.

The best time of year to catch carp on a fly is in the spring when they congregate in huge schools to spawn. Look for muddy areas in shallow water, as well as wakes and even carp trying to jump. (They usually can't because of their immense size.) Once you've located them, you may have a honey hole for several weeks. I have seen them mill around such an area for over a month.

I use a floating line, and my first fly choice is a size 10 lightly weighted brown or rust-colored Woolly Bugger. This pattern not only resembles a number of carp foods, but does not splat on the water like a heavier conehead fly or Clouser Deep Minnow, so it is less likely to alarm the carp. The cloudy water presents some advantages, too. Carp are easier to approach and are less likely to see you cast. However, that cast still must be delicate, even in murky water, because these fish are so easily spooked. When carp are schooled up to spawn, however, the fact that a single cast will present your fly to many carp at a time increases your chances significantly.

No matter how softly your fly lands, because you can't see through the milky water, it is inevitable that occasionally you will cast on top of fish, sending the entire school running in all directions. Don't panic when this happens. These carp are here for a reason, and generally they quickly settle down and return. I leave my fly where it landed for several minutes or until I see a tail or swirl of a carp near it, then I begin to retrieve. The slowest retrieve imaginable works best. I strip in only an inch or so every 10 seconds. Remember, carp eat a lot of vegetation, which doesn't move, and their other food sources, insect larvae and crayfish, don't move much until the last second when threatened by a predator.

The summer, when spawning is finished, is the most rewarding time of year to fly fish for carp. This is when sight casting to individuals or small groups nudging along the bottom in 2 feet of water or parting grass on a flooded bank raises the adrenaline of even the snootiest trout angler. Finding them however, requires a bit of experience.

If you fish a particular lake regularly, you may have a spot in mind where you have seen carp before, and staking them out until they arrive is a good method. But carp are roamers, and sometimes a slow, observant walk along the shoreline works best. One of the easiest indications of feeding carp is to spot a cloudy or muddy spot, (a mud) in otherwise clear water. Most often, one or two carp are creating the mud while feeding along the bottom. Watch the mud to determine the direction in which the mudding carp are moving. Begin casting slightly ahead of the mud. Remember, there may be unseen carp foraging ahead. Finally, cast right into the mud, let the fly settle, and start slowly stripping. Chances are that one will eat your fly, figuring that it is some type of creature that has been kicked up.

The common carp is a tough customer on a fly rod and can be found throughout the world.

Searching for tailing carp is another method of finding them. Tailing occurs when a carp's tail sticks out of the water as it feeds off the bottom. A tailing carp is a feeding carp, but tailing fish are in a vulnerable position, and don't think they don't know it. They are easy to spook, so you should plan your tactics carefully. Remember that there might be another fish feeding nearby that isn't tailing and that you don't see. Study the situation. A sloppy cast is enough to send them running. The sight of a tailing carp is an exciting one and can cause even the finest fly fishers to act too hastily. Determine the direction in which the fish is heading. Chances are that a good cast that leads the fish slightly will end with a strike.

Carp can also be found feeding on the surface. Aquatic insect hatches can blanket the surface of a lake on a cool summer evening, and hordes of terrestrial beetles, ants, and grasshoppers, along with plant seeds, can accumulate on the surface after a windy day. All of these are foods for carp. Again, approach with stealth. Identify the direction in which the feeding carp are moving and lead the fish by at least 10 feet. A long leader will separate the fly from the shadow of the fly line.

Carp have extremely well-developed senses. They are crafty and intelligent fish that scrutinize not only any artificial that you may present, but their natural foods, as well. They are commonly found in urbanized areas, places where other warmwater fish are not present. Fly fishers should not consider them junk fish, but rather should take advantage of the great sport they offer with a fly rod.

OTHER UNIQUE SPECIES FOR THE FLY

The fifteen different species discussed here could keep any angler content for a long time, but remember that there are a lot more species commonly found in North America that can be taken on fly. If you really want a challenge, try to fool a spotted gar lurking in a deep canal, or a bowfin from a stagnant, murky backwater. Both of these fish add a new dimension to the term "spooky." And of course, there are even more challenges to be found for those who pursue warmwater species with a fly rod throughout the rest of the world—exotic species that only now are beginning to be taken on the fly.

Sauger - Spots on the soft dorsal fin separate this species from the walleye.

Rockbass

The often-disrespected bowfin patrols the stagnant dead end of a canal.

The shocking teeth of this Venezuelan payara explains why piranha are one of their favorite foods.

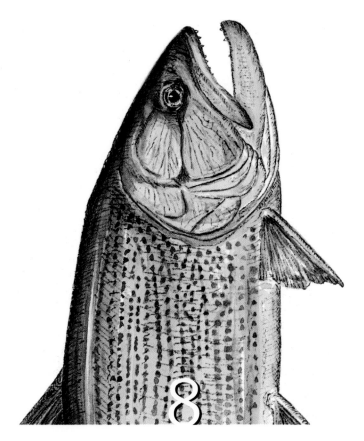

EXOTIC WARMWATER SPECIES

Wherever you visit or travel, if there is fresh water, there is potential for warmwater fly fishing. What follows is a list of ten significant warmwater gamefish species found in exotic locations outside North America, along with color illustrations so you can identify them immediately. Listed with each species are some important facts, their range, the water types in which they reside, size, habitat preference, food preferences, handling concerns, recommended tackle, and three effective fly patterns used to catch them. The section on tactics is left out, because I have not conquered several of these fish myself. Also, developing your own tactics is what keeps this great sport of warmwater fly fishing fun and interesting. I have given a brief overview of the species, though, so that should you find you have an opportunity to pursue these exotic gamefish, you'll have some idea what they're like.

CENTRAL AMERICA

The Guapote Blanco (Guapote or Rainbow Bass)

Notes: A favorite Central American freshwater gamefish, the guapote is best known for its fighting ability and unique and beautiful appearance.

Range: Native from eastern Honduras throughout Nicaragua and Costa Rica and in the northern reaches of Panama.

Water Types: Lakes and rivers.

Size: Commonly reaches 16 inches and 2 pounds, but specimens of up to 12 pounds have been recorded.

Habitat Preference: Water from 5 to 20 feet deep, usually within the vicinity of a sunken tree or brush pile.

Food Preferences: The guapote will eat almost any moving creature of the correct size. This includes small fish, crustaceans, insects, frogs, lizards, and mice.

Handling Concerns: Beware of large, sharp teeth and powerful jaws. Avoid the spines in the dorsal and anal fins.

Close Cousins: The guapote blanco is a member of the enormous Cichlidae family. Its closest cousins are the yellowjacket cichlid, the jaguar guapote, and the green guapote. After much freshwater fishing in Central America, I believe that there are more species of guapote that have not yet been identified, for I have caught them myself.

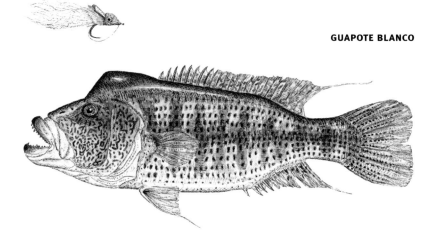

GUAPOTE BLANCO

Recommended Tackle: (based on a 16-inch, 2-pound guapote).

Rod: 9-foot for an 8-weight line.

Reel: Long runs are rare, but a reel with a strong, smooth drag is a must to keep any guapote from retreating to the fortress in which it lives.

Line: 8-weight, weight-forward, floating—WF8F.

Leader: Type B, 7 1/2-foot, 15-pound class tippet and 40 pound mono shock tippet.

Flies: The best hook sizes are from 1/0 to 4. Patterns are the Standard Popper, Prism Diver, and the Clouser Deep Minnow.

The Machaca

Notes: The machaca is a hard fighter known for fierce runs and acrobatic leaps.

Range: Found in Guatemala, El Salvador, Honduras, Nicaragua, Costa Rica, and Panama.

Water Types: Lakes and rivers.

Size: Machaca average around 1 to 2 pounds, with fish up to 5 pounds taken on occasion. The chances of a 10-pounder do exist in the many remote areas in which the machaca is found.

Habitat Preference: In the shade of overhanging trees and other vegetation.

Food Preferences: The machaca is mainly herbivorous, waiting for fruits, seeds, flower petals, and even leaves to fall to the water. However like most warmwater gamefish, the machaca rarely passes up an easy meal and eats insects and minnows with regularity.

MACHACA

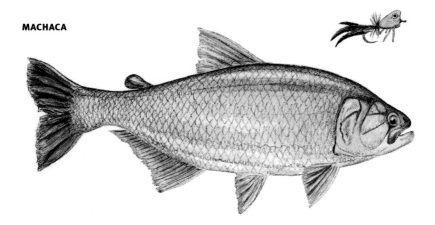

Handling Concerns: Beware of rigid, molarlike teeth.

Close Cousins: The machaca is a member of the Characidae family, which consists of some eight hundred species. The closest relative to the machaca is the matrincha of Brazil.

Recommended Tackle: (based on a 2-pound machaca).

> **Rod:** 9-foot for a 7-weight line.
>
> **Reel:** A sizzling run begins every machaca hookup. A reel with a smooth drag will help prevent a sudden break-off.
>
> **Line:** 8-weight, weight-forward, floating—WF8F.
>
> **Leader:** Type B, 7 1/2-foot, 15-pound class tippet and 40-pound mono shock tippet.
>
> **Flies:** The best hook sizes are from 2 to 6. Patterns are the Standard Popper, Clouser Deep Minnow, and Sanchez's Conehead the Barbarian.

SOUTH AMERICA

The Pavón (Peacock Bass, Tucunaré, Temensis, or Pavón Cinchado)

Notes: The pavón is best known as one of the world's strongest fighting freshwater fish. When landed it is admired for its amazing beauty.

Range: Native to all of northern South America, as well as to the Amazon drainage of Peru, Bolivia, Paraguay, and Brazil. Pavóns have been stocked in the Panama Canal and Lake Gatun of Panama, as well as in Puerto Rico, the Dominican Republic, Guam, the southern reaches of Florida, and Hawaii.

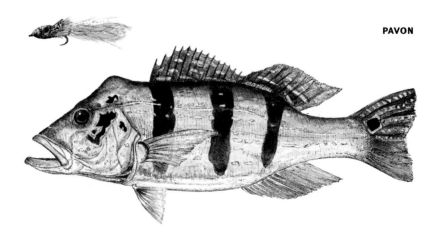

PAVON

Water Types: Lakes, rivers, and canals.

Size: Fish of 4 pounds are common throughout the pavóns native range, with 10-pounders by no means extraordinary. In the remote regions of Venezuela, Columbia, and Brazil, pavón of 20 pounds or more are taken.

Habitat Preference: Water from 5 to 20 feet deep, usually within the vicinity of structure such as logs, trees, brush, or overhanging vegetation.

Food Preferences: If it moves, a pavón will attack it. Pavón are perhaps the most aggressive feeders of all warmwater species. Minnows, small fish, insects, lizards, turtles, frogs, snakes, as well as small mammals and birds are all fair game.

Handling Concerns: Avoid the spines in the dorsal and anal fins.

Close Cousins: The pavón is a member of the enormous Cichlidae family. Its closest relatives are the pavón real (blackstripe peacock bass) and the pavón mariposa (butterfly peacock bass).

Recommended Tackle: (based on a 10-pound pavón).

    Rod: 9-foot for a 10-weight line.

    Reel: Long runs are rare, but a reel with a strong, smooth drag is a must to keep a pavón from retreating to the fortress in which it lives.

    Line: 10-weight, weight-forward, floating—WF10F.

    Leader: Type B, 7 1/2-foot, 20-pound class tippet and 40-pound mono shock tippet.

    Flies: The best hook sizes are from 5/0 to 2/0. Patterns are the Standard Popper, the Prism Diver, and the Clouser Deep Minnow.

The Black Piranha

Notes: Few anglers specifically target the black piranha or any of the many species of piranha. However, when seeking more popular gamefish such as the pavón, they are taken accidentally. On light tackle, piranhas provide an excellent battle, and schooling piranhas can provide hours of action.

Range: All of northern South America including the Orinoco River drainage of Venezuela, as well as the Amazon River drainage from Peru to Brazil and the Parana River drainage of northern Argentina. On rare occasions, unwanted pet piranhas that were illegally introduced have been taken from U.S. waters.

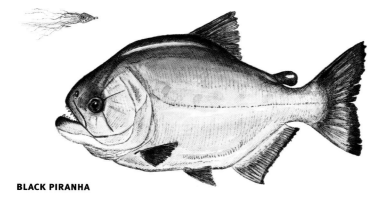

BLACK PIRANHA

Water Types: Rivers, lakes, and ponds.

Size: Most piranha species rarely exceed 2 pounds, but the black piranha is the largest. It commonly surpasses 3 pounds and is believed to surmount 10 pounds.

Habitat Preference: A swarm of piranhas have little fear. Although they are often found near structure, they can just as easily be caught roaming the open water of a large river.

Food Preferences: Individuals prey on smaller fishes and insects, but schools of piranhas will team up and devour an injured or dead animal.

Handling Concerns: Beware of razor-sharp teeth. Always remove your fly with needle-nosed pliers.

Close Cousins: The black piranha is part of the Characidae family, which consists of some eight hundred species. There are several other noteworthy piranha species to target with a fly rod: the red-bellied piranha, the black-spot piranha, the white piranha, and the pirambeba.

Recommended Tackle: (based on a 2-pound black piranha).

    Rod: 9-foot for a 6-weight line.

    Reel: Piranhas fight like bluegills. A reel with a dual-pawl or single-pawl drag system is sufficient.

    Line: 6-weight, weight-forward, floating—WF6F.

    Leader: Type C, 7 1/2-foot, 10-pound class tippet and 40-pound wire bite tippet.

    Flies: The best hook sizes are from 2/0 to 4. Patterns are the Lefty's Deceiver, Clouser Deep Minnow, and Sanchez's Conehead the Barbarian. Your flies will be destroyed by these fish—one fly, one fish. Bring lots of extras.

The Payara (Saber-Toothed Dogfish, Dracula)

Notes: Often overshadowed by the pavón, the payara is another of the great fighters among freshwater gamefish, specializing in long runs and acrobatic performances. The payara thrives in the fast water of jungle rivers. It is best known for its startling appearance, with protruding Dracula-like teeth, including two enormous bottom fangs.

Range: Commonly found throughout Venezuela and other northern South American countries. A smaller species is also found within the Amazon drainage of Brazil and Bolivia.

Water Types: Rivers and occasionally lakes.

Size: Because of their fierce fighting ability, most payara caught weigh less than 10 pounds. However, payara up to 20 pounds are common. It's just that few anglers are equipped with the right tackle to land them. In 1996, a 39-pound, 4-ounce all-tackle world-record payara was taken from a remote Venezuela river.

Habitat Preference: The swift-flowing current of rivers, rapids, and below waterfalls, within the proximity of large rocks.

Food Preferences: Any creature that moves within the payara's sight, especially minnows and other fish that share its habitat, including piranha and the occasional pavón.

Handling Concerns: By all means keep your hands clear of the paraya's fearsome teeth. Always remove your fly with needle-nosed pliers.

Close Cousins: The payara is a member of the Cinodontidae family. It has no close relatives, but is a fish of its own kind.

PAYARA

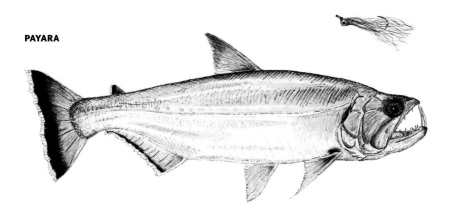

Recommended Tackle: (based on a 10-pound payara).

> **Rod:** 9-foot for a 10-weight line.
>
> **Reel:** Mix the amazing strength of the payara with fast-moving current, and it's obvious that a reel with a strong, smooth drag and capacity for at least 100 yards of 30-pound backing is required.
>
> **Line:** 10-weight, weight-forward, sinking—WF10S.
>
> **Leader:** Type C, 7 1/2-foot, 20-pound class tippet and 40-pound wire bite tippet.
>
> **Flies:** Big flies are best. The best hook sizes are from 5/0 to 2/0. Patterns are the Prism Diver, the Clouser Deep Minnow, and the Sanchez Double Bunny. Flies will be destroyed by these fish—one fly, one fish. Bring lots of extras.

The Freshwater Dorado (Golden Dorado or Picudo)

Notes: The dorado is perhaps the finest of South American freshwater gamefish. It is best known for its arm-jolting strikes, aerial performances, and ferocious fighting ability. It has jaws like a bear trap and has been known to crush the hooks of large flies.

FRESHWATER DORADO

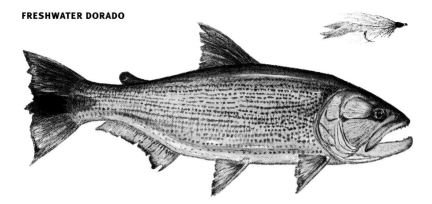

Range: The dorado is most common throughout northern Argentina, Uruguay, Paraguay, Bolivia, and Brazil. However, it has been reported in the Magdalena River system of Colombia and the Orinoco River in Venezuela.

Water Types: Rivers.

Size: Average size is 6 pounds, but 10-pound dorado are common. A 20-pound monster is not unheard of, and the all-tackle world record is 51 pounds, 5 ounces.

Habitat Preference: Fast-flowing rivers with plenty of riffles and rock piles.

Food Preferences: The dorado mainly feeds on other fish, but it is unlikely that any easy meal venturing in the water would be refused, including birds, animals, or large insects.

Handling Concerns: Beware of the strong, toothy jaws. Always remove your fly with needle-nosed pliers.

Close Cousins: The freshwater dorado is a part of the Characidae family, which consists of some eight hundred species. Its closest relative is the tigerfish of Africa.

Recommended Tackle: (based on a 10-pound dorado).

> **Rod:** 9-foot for a 10-weight line.
>
> **Reel:** A reel with a strong, smooth drag is a must, as well as capacity for 200 yards of 30-pound backing.
>
> **Line:** 10-weight, weight-forward, sinking—WF10S.
>
> **Leader:** Type C, 7 1/2-foot, 20-pound class tippet and 40-pound wire bite tippet.
>
> **Flies:** The best hook sizes are from 6/0 to 2/0. Patterns are the Lefty's Deceiver, the Sanchez Double Bunny, and the Clouser Deep Minnow.

AFRICA

The Common Tigerfish

Notes: The common tigerfish is fast becoming the most popular African freshwater gamefish. It is best know for its startling appearance, which features a mouth full of razor-sharp teeth. The common tigerfish is famous for its fine fighting ability, with both bulldogging and many leaps as part of its arsenal.

Range: Throughout much of central and southern Africa, from the southern reaches of the Nile River to the Zambezi River system of Zimbabwe.

Water Types: Rivers and lakes.

Size: An average common tigerfish weighs 4 pounds, but specimens exceeding 10 pounds are caught regularly. They have been known to surpass 20 pounds on rare occasions.

Habitat Preference: In rivers, the common tigerfish holds behind rocks, logs, or other types of debris that form riffles or back eddies. In lakes, they frequently roam in open water in large schools.

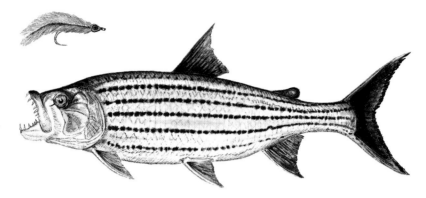

COMMON TIGERFISH

Food Preferences: Other fishes, sometimes nearly half their own body size.

Handling Concerns: Beware of the razor-sharp teeth. Always remove your fly with needle-nosed pliers.

Close Cousins: The common tigerfish is a member of the Characidae family, which consists of some eight hundred species. There is one other tigerfish in Africa, the giant or Goliath tigerfish, which grows to 100 pounds. The closest relative of the tigerfish is the freshwater dorado of South America.

Recommended Tackle: (based on an 8-pound common tigerfish).
Rod: 9-foot for a 9-weight line.
Reel: A reel with a strong, smooth drag is a must, and capacity for 75 yards of 20-pound backing is essential when a tigerfish is hooked in fast current.
Line: 9-weight, weight-forward, floating—WF9F.
Leader: Type C, 7 1/2-foot, 20-pound class tippet and 40-pound wire bite tippet.
Flies: The best hook sizes are from 4/0 to 1/0. Patterns are the Clouser Deep Minnow, the Sanchez Double Bunny, and the Lefty's Deceiver. Flies will be destroyed by these fish—one fly, one fish. Bring lots of extras.

AUSTRALIA

The Murray Cod

Notes: The Murray cod is the largest of Australia's freshwater game-fish. Although not known for great fighting capabilities, the Murray cod battles long and hard.

Range: Throughout parts of the Australian states of Victoria, South Australia, New South Wales, and southern Queensland, particularly in the Murray River drainage.

Water Types: Rivers and lakes.

Size: The Murray cod once exceeded 50 pounds with regularity, and 100-pounders were not unheard-of, but because of declines in habitat, an average catch is less than 20 pounds.

Habitat Preference: The Murray cod prefers slow-flowing current, deep pools, and large back eddies in rivers. In lakes, it hides amid structure such as submerged trees, rocks, and weeds.

Food Preferences: Anything is fair game to a mature Murray cod. Although smaller fish make up the majority of its diet, insects, crayfish, mollusks, frogs, mice, and birds have been found in their stomachs.

Handling Concerns: Avoid the spines in the dorsal and anal fins.

Close Cousins: The Murray cod is a member of the Percichthyidae family. Its closest relatives are the trout cod and the freshwater cod, also of Australia.

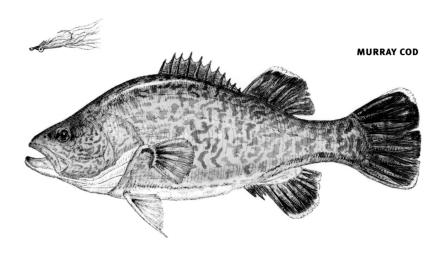

MURRAY COD

Recommended Tackle: (based on a 6-pound Murray cod).
> **Rod:** 9-foot for an 8-weight line.
> **Reel:** Long runs are rare, but a reel with a strong, smooth drag will help stop the powerful Murray cod from retreating to nearby structure.
> **Line:** 8-weight, weight-forward, floating—WF8F.
> **Leader:** Type A, 7 1/2-foot, 16-pound tippet.
> **Flies:** The best hook sizes are from 3/0 to 2. Patterns are the Clouser Deep Minnow, the Sanchez Double Bunny, and the Sanchez Crawdaddy.

The Australian Bass

Notes: One of the most popular freshwater gamefish of Australia, the Australian bass is known for its tough fighting capabilities and ferocious attacks on top-water flies.

Range: Throughout the eastern states of Australia, from southern Queensland to central Victoria.

Water Types: Rivers and lakes.

Size: The Australian bass commonly reaches 2 pounds, but 8-pounders are caught in some lakes with regularity.

Habitat Preference: Australian bass love to hide among the thickest types of structure. Weeds, submerged trees, and roots provide refuge.

Food Preferences: Australian bass are opportunists. Insects, crayfish, smaller fish, mice, birds, lizards, and any other creature that is of edible size that ventures carelessly to the water will likely fall victim to these aggressive feeders.

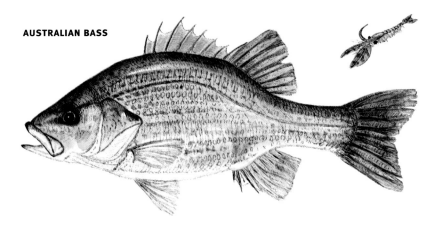

AUSTRALIAN BASS

Handling Concerns: Avoid the spines in the dorsal and anal fins.

Close Cousins: The Australian bass is a member of the Percichthyidae family. Its closest relative is the golden perch, also of Australia.

Recommended Tackle: (based on a 2-pound Australian bass).

> **Rod:** 9-foot for a 7-weight line.
>
> **Reel:** Australian bass do not make screaming long runs, but these fish are brawny fighters. A reel with a strong, smooth drag will help when they try to retreat home.
>
> **Line:** 7-weight, weight-forward, floating—WF7F.
>
> **Leader:** Type A, 7 1/2-foot, 12-pound tippet.
>
> **Flies:** The best hook sizes are from 2 to 6. Patterns are the Standard Popper, the Clouser Deep Minnow, and the Sanchez Crawdaddy.

ASIA

The Mahseer

Notes: The mahseer is the largest member of the carp family and perhaps the least known in the Western world. There are at least several species of mahseer, but exactly how many is unknown. What is known is that the mahseer is not only one of the biggest, but also one of the toughest fighters of all freshwater gamefish. It's also known to be as spooky and difficult to fool as any fish in the world.

Range: Throughout the Himalayas within Pakistan, Afghanistan, Nepal, Bhutan, India, and Bangladesh.

Water Types: Rivers and lakes.

Size: An average catch runs between 10 and 20 pounds, but mahseer can exceed 100 pounds. It has been reported at over 400 pounds in parts of India.

Habitat Preference: Back eddies bordering fast-flowing current and deep holes below rapids. Mahseer can also be found in the open waters of lakes.

Food Preferences: Plants, insects, smaller fish, mollusks, and crabs.

Handling Concerns: Be careful with the mahseer. Large mahseer cannot support their massive body weight out of the water. Don't pick them up by the mouth or gills, because they will literally tear apart.

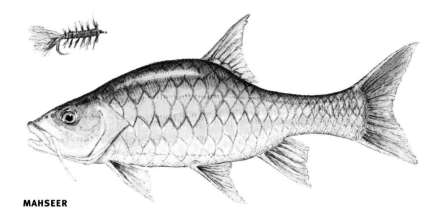

MAHSEER

Close Cousins: The mahseer is part of the Cyprinidae family. Its
closest cousin is the common carp.

Recommended Tackle: (based on a 20-pound mahseer).

Rod: 9-foot for a 10-weight line.

Reel: Your reel must have the strongest, smoothest drag possible and a capacity to hold absolutely no less than 300 yards
of 30-pound backing.

Line: 10-weight, weight-forward, floating—WF10F.

Leader: Type A, 9-foot, 16-pound tippet.

Flies: The best hook sizes are from 2 to 1/0. Patterns are the
Woolly Bugger, the Lefty's Deceiver, and the Sanchez Double
Bunny. It is believed that the mahseer often spooks just from
seeing the hook, so patterns should be tied to hide as much
of the hook shank as possible.

APPENDIX A

WARMWATER EQUIPMENT CHECKLIST

The following checklist represents the absolute minimum equipment that you should carry on a warmwater fly fishing trip. You may want to add other items depending on your destination and the specific demands of that destination.

- [ ] Rods (Take more than one.)
- [ ] Reels
- [ ] Lines (Make sure you have at least one that floats and one that sinks.)
- [ ] Leaders in appropriate sizes and styles (Include extra tippet material in the appropriate sizes and style. Will you need shock tippets? Put 'em in.)
- [ ] Hook sharpener
- [ ] Appropriate flies (If you tie, bring a fly tying kit.)
- [ ] Appropriate footwear (Waders, hip boots, or wading shoes and fast-drying pants.)
- [ ] Vest, fanny pack, daypack, or some other suitable way to carry your gear
- [ ] Hat (Be sure it has a good visor to help visibility on the water and to protect you from the sun.)
- [ ] Warm, quick-drying hat or rain hat
- [ ] Rain gear, even in the tropics
- [ ] Long underwear (tops and bottoms) in northern climates
- [ ] Quick-drying long pants (Supplex is good.)
- [ ] Quick-drying shirts. (In warm climates, wear light, reflective colors.)
- [ ] Shorts
- [ ] Sun screen (Use it frequently.)
- [ ] Polarized sunglasses
- [ ] Line clippers
- [ ] Flashlight
- [ ] Insect repellent
- [ ] First-aid kit
- [ ] Pliers or universal tool
- [ ] Water bottle (In some locations, add a purification device.)
- [ ] Passport if you go anywhere outside the United States

And last, but not least,

- [ ] Currier's Quick and Easy Guide to Warmwater Fly Fishing!

APPENDIX B

JEFF'S FLY BOX

When I began fly fishing in warm water, there were only a handful of patterns specifically designed for warmwater species. With these few patterns, an array of trout flies, and some concoctions of my own, I could fool most of the popular warmwater fish.

Today, the list of warmwater patterns has grown immensely. For example, just within the category of crayfish and frog patterns, there are hundreds of choices. Most of these patterns are excellent, but for the novice warmwater angler, the variety can be overwhelming.

Following is a list of 20 fly patterns and the recipes to tie them, including the colors and sizes of each that I carry in my warmwater fly box at all times. These are mostly common patterns, available at many fly shops, or, if you tie flies, fun to tie. If you start with this selection of proven patterns as a base, you can fine tune your fly selection with other patterns that address specific situations.

POPPERS

STANDARD POPPER

HOOK: Straight eye, wide gape, sizes 6 to 14
THREAD: Yellow, 3/0
WEED GUARD: 10-pound to 20-pound mono
TAIL: Yellow saddle hackles
COLLAR: Orange saddle wrapped 4 times
BODY: Painted foam
EYES: Painted
LEGS: Medium white rubber legs
OTHER COLORS: Any

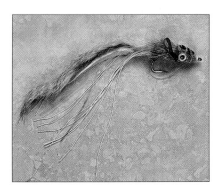

PRISM DIVER SHAD

HOOK: Straight eye, wide gape, sizes 2/0 to 2
THREAD: Red Gudebrod G, or A monocord
WEED GUARD: 15-pound to 25-pound mono
TAIL: Gray rabbit strip, white rubber legs, and pearl Flashabou
COLLAR: Prism tape glued with Goop over a thin piece of red foam
BODY: Clipped spun natural and blue deer hair (Add your own choices of color.)
GILLS: Clipped spun red deer hair
EYES: Doll eyes glued on with superglue
OTHER COLORS: Black, chartreuse, yellow, white, etc.

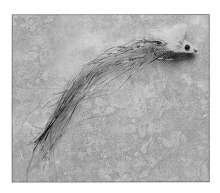

DAHLBERG MEGA DIVER

HOOK: Straight eye, wide gape, size 1/0
THREAD: Chartreuse, 3/0
WEED GUARD: 15-pound to 25-pound mono, or 10-pound to 20-pound solid wire
TAIL: Chartreuse Big Fly Fiber and gold Flashabou
COLLAR: Clipped spun chartreuse deer hair
BODY: Clipped spun chartreuse deer hair
EYES: Plastic eyes
OTHER COLORS: White, yellow, and black

MOUSE

Mouserat

HOOK: Straight eye, wide gape, size 6

THREAD: Brown, 3/0

WEED GUARD: 15-pound to 25-pound mono

TAIL: Tan chamois (a Zonker strip will work)

BODY: Clipped spun natural deer hair

EARS: Tan chamois

EYES: Black waterproof marking pen

WHISKERS: Natural moose

FROG

Swimming Frog

HOOK: Straight eye, wide gape, sizes 2 to 6

THREAD: Orange, 3/0

WEED GUARD: 15-pound to 25-pound mono

TAIL: Orange grizzly and olive grizzly saddle hackles, two each

COLLAR: Clipped spun green, chartreuse, and orange deer hair

BODY: Clipped spun green, chartreuse, yellow, and black deer hair

LEGS: Large orange and chartreuse rubber legs

EYES: Plastic eyes

INSECTS

SPENT DAMSEL-DRAGON

HOOK: Straight eye, wide gape, sizes 6 to 10
THREAD: White, 3/0
WEED GUARD: 15-pound to 25-pound mono
UNDERBODY: Foam
RIB: Blue thread such as flat waxed nylon
BODY: Dark blue bucktail on the top and light blue bucktail on the bottom
WINGS: Light blue and natural deer hair
EYES: Doll eyes

DAVE'S HOPPER

HOOK: Down eye, 3X or 4X long, sizes 2 to 14
THREAD: Yellow, 6/0
TAIL: Red deer hair and yellow poly yarn
BODY: Yellow poly yarn, palmered with brown hackle, hackle trimmed
WING: Mottled turkey quill coated with Flexament
LEGS: Yellow grizzly hackle stem, trimmed and knotted
HEAD: Clipped spun natural deer hair. Leave some unclipped to form the collar.

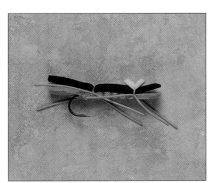

CHERNOBYL ANT

HOOK: Down eye, 3X or 4X long, sizes 4 to 12
THREAD: Tan, 3/0
BODY: Black foam on top, tan foam on bottom
LEGS: Medium black rubber legs
INDICATOR: White foam

NYMPHS

BEADHEAD RUBBER-LEG HARE'S EAR

HOOK: Down eye, 1X or 2X long, sizes 8 to
18, weighted with a brass bead
THREAD: Brown, 6/0
TAIL: Hare's mask
RIB: Medium gold wire
BODY: Dubbed hare's mask or hare's ear
dubbing
LEGS: Pumpkin Sili Legs

BEADHEAD RUBBER-LEG KAUFMANN STONE

(This is an excellent hellegrammite pattern.)
HOOK: Down eye, sizes 2 to 12, weighted
with a brass bead and lead wire
THREAD: Black, 3/0
TAIL: Black biot
RIB: Black Swannundaze
LEGS: Medium black rubber legs
BODY: Black dubbing
WING CASE: Black turkey
ANTENNAE: Black turkey biot
OTHER COLORS: Brown, tan

SANCHEZ SUNFISH DAMSEL NYMPH

HOOK: Down eye, 2X or 3X, sizes 6 to 12,
weighted with a silver bead
THREAD: Chartreuse, 3/0
TAIL: Olive rabbit hair
RIB: Chartreuse thread or floss
BODY: Olive rabbit fur dubbing
WING CASE: Tuft of rabbit hair
LEGS: Medium chartreuse rubber legs
OTHER COLORS: Chartreuse, yellow,
and black.

BAITFISH

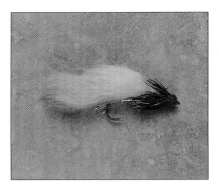

KIWI MUDDLER
HOOK: Down eye, 3X long, sizes 2 to 12, weighted with lead wire
THREAD: White, 3/0
BODY: Pearl Mylar tubing
WING: Rabbit with pearl Krystal Flash
HEAD: Clipped spun natural deer hair. Leave some unclipped to form collar.
OTHER COLORS: Natural gray, chinchilla, brown, black, yellow, etc.

CLOUSER DEEP MINNOW
HOOK: Straight eye, 3X or 4X long, sizes 2/0 to 10
THREAD: Chartreuse, 3/0
EYES: Painted dumbbell eyes
WING: Yellow and chartreuse bucktail with strands of gold Krystal Flash
OTHER COLORS: Chartreuse/white, red/white, brown/orange, olive/gold, etc.

SANCHEZ'S CONEHEAD THE BARBARIAN
HOOK: Straight eye, 4X long, sizes 2/0 to 4, weighted with a conehead
THREAD: Red, 3/0
WING: Gray saddle hackles with pearl Krystal Flash
THROAT: Red Flashabou
HEAD: Large conehead with prism tape wrapped over and trimmed, then coated with five-minute epoxy or Soft Body
EYES: 3/16 -inch or 1/4 -inch stick-on eyes
OTHER COLORS: Black, brown, chartreuse, white, etc.

LEFTY'S DECEIVER
HOOK: Straight eye, 4X long, sizes 4/0 to 2
THREAD: Red, 3/0
TAIL: White saddle hackles with pearl Krystal Flash
BODY: Tying thread
WING: Red bucktail on top, white bucktail on bottom
THROAT: Red Krystal Flash
EYES: Painted

SANCHEZ DOUBLE BUNNY
HOOK: Straight eye, wide gape, sizes 3/0 to 2, weighted on the front half with lead wire
THREAD: Gray, 3/0
WEED GUARD: 15-pound to 25-pound mono
BODY/WING: Rabbit strips, chartreuse on the top white on the bottom, glued together with leather contact cement
LATERAL LINE: Pearl Krystal Flash
EYES: 5/16-inch stick on eyes
HEAD: Soft Body
OTHER COLORS: Olive/tan, olive/gray, yellow/black, gray/white, etc.

LEECHES

WOOLLY BUGGER

HOOK: Down eye, 3X or 4X long, sizes 2 to 12, weighted with lead wire
THREAD: Black, 3/0
TAIL: Purple marabou with pearl Krystal Flash
RIB: Medium copper wire
BODY: Purple chenille
HACKLE: Black, palmered
OTHER COLORS: Black, olive, brown, white, yellow, chartreuse, etc.

CONEHEAD MOHAIR LEECH

HOOK: Down eye, 3X or 4X long, sizes 2 to 12, weighted with a black conehead and lead wire
THREAD: Black, 3/0
TAIL: Red marabou with copper Krystal Flash
BODY: Blood leech yarn
OTHER COLORS: Black, olive, purple, brown, etc.

CRAYFISH

SANCHEZ CRAWDADDY

HOOK: Down eye, 4X long, sizes 2 to 8, weighted with a copper conehead, with lead wire on the front half of the hook

THREAD: Orange, 3/0

ANTENNAE: Brown rubber legs

RIB: Nymph Rib

BODY: Tan chenille

CARAPACE: Wide orange rabbit strip. This is trimmed to shape and will be tied fur side down. Pull the hair off the hide on the front two-thirds of the carapace. Precoat the rabbit hides with silicone caulking and glitter.

CLAWS: The hair on the rear third of carapace is pulled to the sides before impaling the carapace on the hook point.

LEGS: Three medium brown rubber legs pulled through the carapace with a needle and cemented.

OTHER COLORS: Olive or brown.

WHITLOCK'S SOFTSHELL CRAYFISH

HOOK: Down eye, 6X long, sizes 2 to 8, weighted on the front half with lead wire

THREAD: Orange, 3/0

ANTENNAE: Black moose, peccary, or rubber legs

RIB: Medium copper wire

BODY: Rust dubbing

CARAPACE: Rust Swiss Straw, colored black, olive, or dark brown with a waterproof marking pen

CLAWS: Orange or brown hen saddle. Flexament them together.

LEGS: Rust grizzly saddle hackle

EYES: Melted 20-pound mono (You may use dumbbell eyes.)

NOSE: Orange or brown deer

OTHER COLORS: Olive or brown.

APPENDIX C
JEFF'S TIPS FOR WARMWATER SUCCESS

If you begin with this book and develop a love for warmwater fly fishing, as I have, you will want to learn more. I highly recommend books such as *Fly Fishing for Smallmouth Bass,* by Harry Murray (New York, N.Y.: Lyons Press, 1998); *Carp on the Fly: A Flyfishing Guide,* by Barry Reynolds, Brad Befus, and John Berryman (Boulder, Colo.: Johnson Publishing, 1997); *Pike on the Fly: The Flyfishing Guide to Northerns, Tigers, and Muskies,* by Barry Reynolds and John Berryman (Boulder, Colo.: Johnson Publishing, 1993); and the *L.L. Bean Fly Fishing for Bass Handbook,* by Dave Whitlock (New York, N.Y.: Lyons Press, 1998). You may also enjoy videos by many of these same authors. These all provide extensive information on the sport and include nearly all other knots and techniques not addressed here. Also, see the Bibliography for other helpful references on warmwater fly fishing.

But, as with any pursuit, there are a number of simple techniques, habits, and rules that will enhance your warmwater fly-fishing experience. Follow these tips faithfully and you will have more success, and, consequently, more fun.

TIPS FOR WARMWATER FLY FISHING

• Routinely check your knots, both new and old. A fish should never be lost because of a poor knot.

• Never fish a fly without a razor-sharp hook. A small hook file obtainable from a tackle store is a must. The best procedure is to hold the fly with your pliers and file the hook point in a triangular shape. A sharp hook will stick to your fingernail.

• Always bring insect repellent. I have found that the better my fishing, the more bugs there are to bite me. Put it on ahead of time and wash your hands. Many repellents contain DEET, which eats away at a fly line's finish.

• Always be prepared to cast your best. Distance, speed, and accuracy are important. Learn the double haul. Practice your casting before you go.

• Extra line always seems to tangle around your feet and other objects when you're in a boat. Keep a clean casting deck and don't be afraid to take off your shoes and socks. (Put sunscreen on the tops of your feet.) You'll feel the coils of extra line with your toes and stay off them.

• Never pull a fly away from a feeding fish. It is a common mistake while stripping a wet fly to set the hook when a fish is charging a fly and before it actually takes it. It's like buck fever. If you don't feel the fish, don't set the hook.

• If you plan to purchase new rods for warmwater fly fishing, invest in multiple-piece travel rods. Today, the quality of these rods is equal to that of two-piece rods. Some of the best warmwater destinations require airline travel, and I feel better if my rods are carry-on items.

• Any trip whether it be a honeymoon, anniversary, vacation, or business is a good excuse to take along a fly rod. Don't leave home without one!

BIBLIOGRAPHY

Here is a list of books, videos, and articles that can provide you with more information. These are readings that I often use myself to learn more about all aspects of warmwater fishing.

BOOKS

Currier, Jeff. *Currier's Quick and Easy Guide to Saltwater Fly Fishing.*
Helena, MT: Greycliff Publishing Company, 1998.

Eddy, Samuel and James C. Underhill. *How to Know Freshwater Fishes.*
Dubuque, Iowa: Wm. C. Brown Company Publishers, 1983.

Kaufmann, Randall. *Fly Patterns of Umpqua Feather Merchants.*
Glide, Oreg: Umpqua Feather Merchants, 1998.

Larsen, Larry. *Peacock Bass & Other Fierce Exotics.*
Lakeland, Florida: Larsen's Outdoor Publishing, 1996.

McClane, A. J. *McClane's Field Guide to Freshwater Fishes of North America.*
New York: Holt, Rinehart, and Winston, Inc, 1978.

___, ed. *McClane's New Standard Fishing Encyclopedia.*
New York: Holt, Rinehart, and Winston, 1974.

McClane, A. J. and Keith Gardner. *McClane's Game Fish of North America.*
New York, NY: Times Books, 1984.

Murray, Harry. *Fly Fishing for Smallmouth Bass.*
New York: The Lyons Press, 1989.

Page, M. Lawrence and Brooks M. Burr. *Peterson Field Guide to Freshwater Fishes.* New York: Houghton Mifflin Company, 1991.

Pfeiffer, C. Boyd. *Bug Making.*
New York: Lyons & Burford, Publishers, 1993.

Reynolds, Barry, Brad Befus and John Berryman. *Carp on the Fly.*
Boulder, Colorado: Johnson Publishing Company, 1997.

Reynolds, Barry and John Berryman. *Beyond Trout.*
Boulder, Colorado: Johnson Publishing Company, 1995.

Reynolds, Barry and John Berryman. *Pike on the Fly.*
Boulder, Colorado: Johnson Publishing Company, 1993.

Ryan, Will. *Smallmouth Strategies for the Fly Rod.*
New York: Lyons & Burford, Publishers, 1996.

Shultz, Ken. *Ken Schultz's Fishing Encyclopedia.*
Foster City, CA: IDG Books Worldwide, Inc.

Sosin, Mark and Lefty Kreh. *Practical Fishing Knots II.*

New York: Lyons & Burford, Publishers, 1991.
Stewart, Dick and Farrow Allen. *Flies for Bass & Panfish.*
   North Conway, NH: Mountain Pond Publishing, 1992.
Tinsley, Russell. *Fishing Texas: An Angler's Guide.*
   Fredericksburg, TX: Shearer Publishing, 1988.
Whitlock, Dave. *L.L. Bean Fly Fishing for Bass Handbook.*
   New York: Lyons & Burford, Publishers, 1988.
(11 contributors). *Musky Country.*
   Minocqua, Wisconsin: Willow Creek Press, 1995.

VIDEOS

Dahlberg, Larry. *Flyfishing for Pike.*
   Brainerd, MN: In-Fisherman Communications, 1989.
Whitlock, Dave. *Bass On A Fly Top to Bottom.*
   Fort Worth, Texas: Sports Tapes, 1992.
___, ed. *Flyfishing For Bass.*
   Fort Worth, Texas: Sport Tapes, 1985.

ARTICLES

Elliott, Brook. *"The White (Bass) of Spring."*
   Warmwater Fly Fishing. Spring, 2000.
Fawcett, Joel S. *"White Perch Strategies."*
   Warmwater Fly Fishing. February/March, 1999.
Holschlag, Tim. *"Drumming on the River."*
   Warmwater Fly Fishing. February/March, 1999.
Kantner, Steve. *"The Oscar Option."*
   Warmwater Fly Fishing. April/May, 1999.
King, Ivory A. *"Bass Attack!"*
   Freshwater Fishing Australia Magazine. Issue 37, Summer, 1996.
Morgan, Stephen. *"Bass."*
   Freshwater Fishing Australia Magazine. Issue 29, Summer, 1995.
Shapiro, Oliver. *"Panfish & Poppers."*
   Warmwater Fly Fishing. October/November, 1999.
Stange, Doug. *"Channel Cats—A Case Study."*
   In-Fisherman. February-March, 2000.
Sternberg, Dick. *"Spring Fishing Handbook."*
   Outdoor Life. March, 2000.
Williams, Joseph. *"Stream Tactics for Freshwater Natives."*
   Freshwater Fishing Australia Magazine. Issue 37, Summer 1996.

INDEX